RED & WHITE

Indian Views of the White Man
1492–1982

Annette Rosenstiel

UNIVERSE BOOKS

New York

To the Indians of the Americas
without whose eloquent testimony
this book could never have been written

Published in the United States of America in 1983
by Universe Books
381 Park Avenue South, New York, N.Y. 10016
© 1983 by Annette Rosenstiel

83 84 85 86 87/10 9 8 7 6 5 4 3 2 1

Printed in the United States of America

Library of Congress Cataloging in Publication Data
Main entry under title:

Red and white.

   Bibliography: p.
   Includes index.
   1. Indians of North America—History—Sources.
2. Indians of North America—Government relations—
Sources. 3. Indians of North America—Oratory.
I. Rosenstiel, Annette, 1911-
E77.R4   1983   970.004'97   82-23901
ISBN 0-87663-373-4

Contents

Acknowledgments

Individuals, publishers, and government agencies which have graciously granted permission for reproduction of materials to which they hold the rights have been acknowledged elsewhere in this book.

I wish, however, especially to thank the following for their assistance in the arduous task of finding the most effective textual and illustrative materials to include in the book: Albany Institute of History and Art; Rare Books and Manuscripts Division, The New York Public Library; Associate Director for Special Collection, The New York Public Library; National Anthropological Archives; American Museum of Natural History; The New-York Historical Society; Bibliothèque nationale (Paris); Library of Congress; Smithsonian Institution; Public Archives of Canada; Provincial Archives of Canada; Provincial Archives of Alberta; State Library at Albany; Reference Division, Nassau County Public Library System; Reference Librarians, C. W. Post College (Long Island University); Reference Librarians, Wm. Paterson College (New Jersey); Professor Emeritus Sol Tax of the University of Chicago; John Knox, Piseco Lake, N.Y.; Chief W. W. Red Fox; Shiyowin Miller; The International Indian Treaty Council; and Chief David Courchene.

I have made every effort to locate persons holding rights to any of the materials used in this book. In most cases, written permission has been obtained wherever necessary. However, in a few cases, mail and telephone inquiries have had no positive results. If, therefore, any material has been inadvertently used which requires formal permission, I wish to apologize, and to assure any persons concerned that, in the event that there are future editions of this book, this will be corrected.

Introduction

In 1493 Christopher Columbus announced to the European world that his voyage of discovery the previous year had led him to an uncharted realm filled with exotic flora and fauna of all descriptions—and to a strange and hitherto unsuspected people. In his zeal to convince the Spanish Crown that the natives he had discovered were indeed subjects of the Great Khan, ruler of fabled Cathay—it had been the explorer's mission to find a new sea route to the East Indies—Columbus insisted on calling them "Indians." The name persisted long after everyone knew that what Columbus had found were vast new continents rather than islands bordering China.

Columbus's account of the New World unleashed a tide of exploration and conquest that was destined to change the Americas, and their inhabitants, forever. Lured there by tales of limitless riches, the first Europeans brought with them death and destruction of a magnitude that had been equaled in Europe only during the ravages of the Black Death.

The people of the New World were totally different from any the Europeans had seen before. Shocked and horrified, Spaniards, dressed in layers and layers of silk, wool, cotton, and even armor of mail with steel breastplates and iron helmets, watched thousands of naked men and women, with bodies the color of burnished bronze, lolling about in the tropical sun of the West Indies. Having been raised to spend their lives fully clothed, the Spaniards, and other Europeans who later followed them, concluded that the Indians they had discovered were less than human. Otherwise, they decided, they would have found more complete ways to clothe themselves than the occasional palm fronds, feathers, and other wispy materials with which the natives covered their genitals.

Many Caribbean Indians were hostile to each other, as well as to the Spaniards. Some of the tribes were also known to be cannibals. This further unnerved the Spanish, who did not understand the difference between the Indians' ritual cannibalism, practiced as a means of absorbing the good qualities of captured enemies, or as a testimony of respect to their elders, and indiscriminate killing. Even if the explorers' sense of morality had not been as outraged as it was by these departures from what they believed was the universal morality of civilized nations, they would still have been on the defensive because of their fear of being eaten. From some Indians' penchant for meals of human flesh grew tales of nightmarish proportions among the

Spaniards and later the Portuguese, until it seemed to them that the only thing to do was to strike first at these barbarians who made human sacrifices and ate the flesh of their brothers.

From the 15th century on, the contentious European powers fought each other and the Indians for ever-greater shares of the New World territories and treasures. In those early years of the discovery and conquest of the Americas, the Indians were also considered "treasures." The Europeans took them as slaves, hostages, bearers, guides, concubines, and sometimes even as wives. Often they shipped cargoes of Indians back to Europe to be sold at auction in order to increase the profits or help defray the costs of their expeditions. Throughout the New World many Indians resisted the European onslaught for years, hiding in the dense, lush tropical rainforests and desolate mountain valleys. They used their ingenuity to avoid the Europeans, and when cornered they defended themselves against the cannons, guns, ferocious dogs, horses, and metal armor of the invaders with spears, arrows, primitive shields, and poisons. By the early 17th century, England, France, Portugal, and Spain were vying for supremacy in the New World, and for the ultimate subjugation of the Indians.

Preserved in both words and pictures, the history of the Americas can be seen from both the European and the Indian points of view. Accounts of Indian-white relations have been written by English, Spanish, French, Italian, and German explorers, missionaries, travelers, and social philosophers. The Indian point of view was at first conspicuously absent, but more and more Indian reactions were recorded from the 17th through the 19th centuries by the white men who were gradually coming to appreciate the Indians as thinking, feeling human beings. And, as the Indians became more fluent in the language of their conquerors, they began to record their own reactions and opinions.

During the 20th century, Indians have more frequently than ever before written their own history and spoken out for themselves in public forums.

How did the Indians feel about the Europeans? They were decimated by the murder, rape, and destruction wreaked by the newcomers to their shores. And since they were neither the noble savages depicted by Rousseau nor the implacable, amoral killers described by their worst enemies, the natives of the New World displayed a wide range of emotions and considerable ingenuity as they grappled with the problem of living their own lives in a situation they could no longer control.

A long tradition of eloquent oratory was an outstanding feature of Indian life, and in many tribes there were gifted, articulate individuals who were delegated to speak for their people. But at the beginning—and even for many years thereafter—most of their efforts were frustrated. Indian spokesmen were handicapped at first by their inability to communicate in European languages. Consequently, they were frequently forced to resort to a rude pidgin version of whatever language they were trying to speak, or to an improvised sign language; thus most of their efforts to convey their feelings articulately were frustrated. Even more difficult for both sides were the instances of deliberate mistranslation. "Interpreters," fearing to offend either side, often either simply changed meanings in translation so that each side was told what it presumably wanted to hear rather than what the speaker had said, or deliberately mistranslated what the Indians said, sometimes with disastrous results.

Believing that the Indians were simpletons, for many years the Europeans, and later the Americans, treated them like children, and forced them to acknowledge the whites as their masters. Eventually they herded those who could not or did not choose to flee onto segregated reservations like so many head of cattle. In South America the Jesuits contained many Indians in despotically paternalistic and theocratic villages called *reducciones*. In North America treaties—now considered invalid—between the Indians and the United States government resulted in a profusion of reservations, and in Canada too, Indians were moved onto *réserves* in accordance with treaties now being challenged by the Indians. In all these places the Indians were rendered undereducated for life, no longer proficient in their traditional tribal ways and ignorant of the ways of the white man's world. The process of Europeanization, or Americanization, was never completed, and most Indians remained in a cultural limbo, suspended halfway between the two worlds.

The local caciques (chiefs), those Indians without whom the early explorers and conquerors of the New World could not have carried out their original mission, often realized that their way of life was doomed. They saw all too clearly the Europeans' greed for money, quest for empire, and lust for power. Examples of European kindness were rare indeed. The Indians observed and reported faithfully on Euro-American capriciousness, illogic, and inconsistency, foibles which have changed little over the centuries.

Despite the Europeans' claims of cultural superiority, the Indians had their doubts even in the earliest years of their acquaintance. Later on, the North American Indians saw for themselves the ludicrous results of Anglo-American attempts to teach their youths in boarding schools, far from their homes, families, and traditions. Examples of this were to be found frequently throughout the Americas as the white men sought to "improve" the Indians by changing their outlook on life.

Euro-American society intruded farther and farther into the heartlands of the Americas, leaving the Indians progressively fewer untamed regions in which they could find sanctuary. As their numbers dwindled, it seemed less and less possible that they might be able to preserve even a part of their traditional ways. They had begun to learn enough of the white man's language to be able to argue with him about their plight, but by then it was too late to avoid the social explosion that was bound to follow centuries of conflict, misunderstanding, and emotional pain.

In *Red and White* the Indians speak for themselves. Their revealing comments, scattered in hundreds of isolated sources, hidden away in libraries on three continents, are here collected for the first time. And these excerpts from many documents, letters, books, and speeches show the Indians' presence of mind even in the face of genocide. Their words are trenchant, vivid, and insightful, revealing their strong reactions to the events they witnessed, both in the Americas and in Europe. Throughout the centuries since the Discovery, the Indians have shown us their understanding of the ironies of their situation and of the white man's actions. My search for these insights has taken me to hundreds of documents to be found throughout Europe and the Americas. All English translations from French, German, Italian, Latin, Portuguese, and Spanish are my own, except where otherwise indicated. Statements recorded in English have been standardized in accordance with modern spelling and usage in the interests of clarity and consistency. Nowhere, however, has the meaning of any quotation been modified or changed in any way.

Since the early explorers, missionaries, traders, and others who came to America were from different countries in Europe, tribal names appear in many variant forms in the sources. This initial confusion is further complicated by the fact that early orthography was not standardized. In most cases, in the interest of providing easier comprehension for the general reader, I have used the modern spelling of tribal names in both the text and the quotations—for example, Miamis rather than Ouamis.

Just as I wanted the Indians to speak for themselves, in their own words, so I chose authentic illustrations from each period. Some of these were drawn by Indians; others were sketches made from life by observant European travelers. All the paintings and sketches—and, for more recent events, the photographs—have been chosen for the accuracy of their depiction of the Indians and the situations in which they were involved. Some illustrate the text, while other show analogous or complementary scenes. The Indians are shown in many circumstances unfamiliar to them— among the European aristocracy, visiting large cities, speaking at the white man's festivities—and all the while attempting to preserve their way of life in a changing world.

What did the Indians really think of the Europeans? *Red and White* is the beginning of an answer.

1
The 16th Century
The Gold of the Indies

The Age of Discovery was a time of great turbulence. When Columbus set sail from Palos de la Frontera, Spain, on 3 August 1492, he left behind a country that had only just succeeded in freeing itself from almost eight centuries of Moorish domination. The triumphant entry of the Catholic monarchs, Ferdinand and Isabella, into Granada the preceding January had climaxed a long and costly war which had seriously depleted the royal treasury. The monarchs invested in Columbus's perilous venture in an attempt to replenish their empty coffers.

The rest of Europe was also in turmoil. Protestants were beginning to leave the Roman Catholic Church in large numbers, triggering years of bitterness and bloodshed among rival Christian groups. There was political and economic strife, too, as German princes, the newly centralized kingdom of France, Italian city-states, the Portuguese, the Spaniards, and the English all vied for supremacy in Europe and control of the lucrative overseas trade with other continents.

It was natural that these feuds and conflicts should spread wherever the Europeans traveled. In the 15th and 16th centuries word of vast, unexplored regions was brought back to Europe by the fortunate survivors of hazardous expeditions to those mysterious new lands. Soon, impoverished petty noblemen, ambitious bourgeois traders, and princes of both church and state set out to improve their fortunes by acquiring the reputedly limitless treasures of the New World.

Within a few years after Columbus first reported his discoveries to the Spanish sovereigns, wave after wave of armed Europeans descended on the Americas. First, the Spaniards established a base on the island of Hispaniola (today the Dominican Republic and Haiti), and from there they set out to subdue the surrounding areas. The Europeans had superior force of arms. The natives of the New World were powerless before the cannons and guns of their conquerors.

The Europeans also brought with them terrible scourges—smallpox and other devastating diseases new to the Americas against which the Indians had no resistance. There may have been as many as 80 million Indians in the Americas at the time of the Discovery, but as a result of war, disease, and mistreatment by their European conquerors, as many as 40 million had perished by the mid-16th century.

Spanish cruelty to the Indians was motivated by religious beliefs as well as by greed. The Spaniards wanted the gold and other treasures they believed the natives were keeping from them. But, in addition, the Indian traditions shocked the European sense of propriety. The natives seemed to lack the social refinements that the oversophisticated Europeans considered essential to civilized life. Their languages sounded like gibberish to most travelers, and their practices of homosexuality and ritual cannibalism and human sacrifice were misunderstood and considered "abominations" by the strict Roman Catholic Spaniards, who could not comprehend any religious ritual other than their own. And since this was the era of the Inquisition in Spain, anyone who did not profess Catholicism was automatically considered by the Spaniards to be less than human, deserving no kindness or consideration whatever. All this made it easy for the conquerors to ignore the humanity of the Indians. They had no scruples about enslaving large numbers of them, who were forced to work for their Spanish masters until they dropped from exhaustion. Some were even captured and shipped back to Spain to be sold as slaves there.

As more and more Spaniards came to the New World, they brought the practices of the Inquisition with them. Often they insisted that the Indians embrace Christianity, "encouraging" reluctant converts with physical torture as well as with vivid tales of the fire and brimstone that awaited them in the hereafter if they should persist in their "evil," "barbarous" ways. As a result of Spanish oppression and cruelty, the Indians became bitterly hostile to newly arriving Europeans. This led the Spanish explorers to say of new territories, "If the Indians are friendly, no European has ever been here."

From the beginning, even before any systematic enslavement of the Indians, the Europeans considered America's natives such exotic creatures that they felt constrained to take a few back with them, just to prove that their fantastic stories of the New World were true. Columbus was the first explorer to keep some record of the Indians' reactions to their new experiences. Gradually, other explorers and missionaries began to write about the Indians, too.

But there was still the problem of how to treat them. Although most of the Europeans were willing to write the Indians off as subhuman, Columbus made a small concession to them. He had found that they were indeed capable of learning, and, he declared, they "should make good servants."

Ferdinand and Isabella tried periodically to outlaw the enslavement of the Indians. They ordered that the New World's natives be treated humanely, but most explorers and conquistadors ignored the royal commands. They had braved the dangers of the ocean to get rich—as rich as possible as fast as possible. If it was inconvenient for them to obey the crown's commands, they ignored them. So many thousands of miles from home, who was there to see their cruelty? Who would ever know? So the Spaniards continued to enslave the Indians, to force them to act as translators, porters, and servants on their expeditions, field hands on their sugarcane plantations, and laborers in their gold and silver mines.

Finally, in 1537, Pope Paul III issued a papal bull declaring that the Indians of the New World were indeed human beings—thinking, feeling individuals who were capable of learning right from wrong, and therefore capable of understanding the tenets of Christianity. Consequently, he told his faithful followers, the Indians were not really inferior to the Spaniards, and Europeans loyal to the Church of Rome should cease to mistreat the natives in the areas they explored and colonized. But his orders were not obeyed, any more than those of Ferdinand and Isabella had been.

America's conquerors were often frustrated in their goals. Sometimes they found no treasures, no gold, no silver, no spices. The voyage across the sea was expensive and dangerous. If they returned empty-handed, the sailors and their leaders faced financial ruin. In desperation, at times like those, Spaniards continued to kidnap Indians and send them back to be sold as slaves in Spain in the hope that proceeds from these sales would help repair their diminishing fortunes.

When Estévan Gómez kidnapped Indians in 1525, he sent a large shipload of them back to Spain to be sold into slavery. Meanwhile, Charles I of Spain had, like Ferdinand and Isabella, outlawed Indian slavery, and when it was discovered that Gómez had in fact defied the ban, and that he had brought back slaves, and not spices, as had been supposed, he was ordered to set free all the Indians who had survived the rough Atlantic crossing and to send them back home. In this case, at least, a European monarch put some teeth into his antislavery laws. But such an instance was rare.

The French, with their proverbial aptitude for diplomacy, managed to make themselves as loved and accepted by the Indians as the Spaniards had made themselves feared and hated. In some areas of Brazil, the French were the first to arrive. They established themselves as trustworthy, keeping all their promises to the Indians, and were permitted to pass safely through tribal territories, and even to live among them as traders. The French gave the Indians good quality knives, hatchets, mirrors, combs, and scissors and received in exchange the natives' best Brazilwood, cotton, feathers, and pepper, which they shipped back to France. They endeared themselves so much to the Indians that even those tribes that were known to practice cannibalism did not consider them enemies and refused to harm them.

When the Portuguese (and, until 1640, the Spanish) replaced the French as rulers of Brazil, they were at first welcomed by the Indians, who expected the same kind of amicable relationship with the Portuguese that they had had with the French. However, when delegations of Indians came aboard the Portuguese vessels to trade, they were seized. Some were garrotted; others were sold by the Portuguese to rival Indian tribes who were cannibals, and who then massacred and ate their erstwhile enemies.

The remaining Indians were desperate. As the Portuguese yoke became too much to bear, formerly rival tribes joined forces and attacked their Portuguese tormentors, compelling them to retreat temporarily. And anyone who faintly reminded those Indians of the hated Spanish and Portuguese was likely to find himself in the nearest cooking pot.

The Indians were well aware that their world was slipping away from them, their numbers diminished by persecution and disease, their customs eroding. They understood the difference between the rapacious, gold-hungry Spaniards and the more humane French explorers, but ultimately both were part of the irresistible European onslaught with its attendant forced conversions to Christianity. The Indians recognized that their way of life was being destroyed, and they bewailed the inevitable loss of their identity.

The Caribbean Indian chief Hatuay is burned at the stake for refusing to convert to Christianity. From Girolamo Benzoni, Narratio Regionum . . . *(Oppenheim, 1614). Rare Books and Manuscripts Division, NYPL.*

1511

Caribbean Indians, having learned through bitter experience the Spanish penchant for kidnapping natives and selling them into slavery, were terrified by news of the impending arrival of Spanish ships. In panic, some of them fled into the rain forests in the interior. Others left their own islands and tried desperately to escape enslavement by going from island to island, in a futile attempt to avoid the dreadful fate they knew was in store for them.

One of these Indians, Hatuay, a cacique on the island of Hispaniola, gathered up his family and belongings and fled to Cuba, but was caught by the Spaniards in 1511. Sentenced to be burned alive at the stake for the "crime" of refusing to be converted to Christianity, he was given one last chance to save his soul. As Hatuay stood bound to the stake, a Franciscan friar promised him eternal bliss in exchange for his conversion to Roman Catholicism. Painting a graphic picture of the tortures that awaited Hatuay in hell, should he refuse to convert, the friar awaited the chief's decision.

Were there any Spaniards in heaven? Hatuay inquired calmly. There most certainly were, the friar assured him. At the prospect of spending all eternity with the same people who had condemned him to death, Hatuay exclaimed:

> I will not go to a place
> where I may meet with one
> of that accursed race!

Comagre's son Ponciaco shows his disgust with the greed of Balboa's men, who have begun to fight over the finely wrought golden ornaments Comagre has given them. Reproduced from the Collections of the Library of Congress.

1516

Indian tradition demanded that friendly strangers be given hospitality, and at first the conquistadors were received openhandedly. Learning that the newcomers loved gold above all else, the Indians willingly shared what they had with the Europeans.

When Vasco Nuñez de Balboa slashed his way across the wild Panamanian rain forests in his quest for the ocean beyond, he was befriended by a tribe that had never before met any Europeans. When the Spaniards prepared to continue their journey, Comagre, their cacique, and his sons, offered the Spaniards a magnificent parting gift—four thousand ounces of gold.

These Indians, who panned gold from open streams and to whom it was an adornment rather than an obsession, soon saw an ugly spectacle. The newcomers began brawling among themselves, arguing about the division of the gold. Comagre's eldest son, Ponciaco, disgusted with the Spaniards' behavior, knocked to the ground the scales they had been using, scattering the gold in all directions, and demanded angrily:

> What is the matter, you Christian men, that you esteem a little bit of gold so much more than your own peace of mind? . . . If your desire for gold is so insatiable that merely for the desire of it you disturb so many people . . . I will show you a region flowing with gold, where you may satisfy your appetites.

15

As the Mayan Jaguar priests had foretold, the Spanish army soon overran their country, devastating the land and forcing the Indians to become their slaves. From Codex Azcatitlán. *Bibliothèque nationale, Paris.*

1517

In tropical Yucatan, the Spaniards faced a long and bitter struggle with the Mayan Indians, who resisted them subtly as well as openly. Soon after the Spanish first arrived, the Jaguar priests, or *Chilam Balam*—soothsayers who foretold mysterious or hidden things—declared that they foresaw the horrors that would come with the arrival of more Europeans. When the use of Mayan hieroglyphs was forbidden by the Spanish and most of their sacred books were burned, the priests dictated their predictions to a bilingual scribe who set them down in Maya, but written in European script. In this way the priests preserved for posterity their vision of the Spaniards as harbingers of destruction.

> The Spanish will soon take possession. They will bring to pass the final days and the end of all protection of the people. . . . Men with trumpets are making the rounds of the country. . . . Then come the men to dig to the very bottom to fill their baskets. They lay waste the property of our peoples, making destitute the houses of rulers. . . . The offenses of the white people are all alike, even against those who surrender themselves or their enemies. Brothers plead for justice in their throats. Gradually we discover that the Christians are great liars. Little by little we realize that they are cheats.

While the Indians try in vain to protect themselves against the onslaught of the heavily armed Spanish soldiers, priests are everywhere, even on the battlefield, trying to convert the hapless natives to Christianity. From Theodor de Bry, Historia Americae *(Frankfurt, 1590). Rare Books and Manuscripts Division, NYPL.*

1517

In the disguised Mayan script used after the Spanish forbade the Indians to write their traditional language, the Jaguar priests were able to record the activities of their conquerors and their devastating effect on Mayan civilization. As eager as the conquistadors were to strip the Indians of their lands and treasures, their zeal was equaled by that of the missionaries, who were avid to persuade the natives to convert to Christianity for the sake of their immortal souls. The Mayans have passed on to us a history of forced conversion and the death of an old order.

> The bearded ones, the ones who shoot—this is the signal of the white God—were arriving. Six sons of heaven, some aged and infirm, came shouting to announce the news, spreading it over the country. They were present in every clump of trees, behind every heap of rocks, the friars, all exactly alike in appearance, negotiating for our souls and haranguing us about the "true God."

When the Aztecs came to greet the Spaniards under Cortés, they tried to board Spanish ships, only to be greeted with volleys of frightening gunfire. From Bernardino de Sahagún, The Florentine Codex: General History of the Things of New Spain, *trans. Arthur J. O. Anderson and Charles E. Dibble (Santa Fe, N.M., 1950–59), bk. 12.*

1519

The Aztecs had myths telling of a blond race of gods who would come to them from over the sea: Quetzalcoatl, the legendary creator of the Aztec culture, had been driven away by his evil brother Tezcatlipoca, but he had promised to return, and with him would come a time of peace and plenty. When the fair-haired Spaniard Hernando Cortés and his forces arrived in Mexico, Montezuma, the Aztec ruler, mistook them for the returning Quetzalcoatl and his retinue, and believed that the promised era of plenitude had begun.

When he appeared, Cortés was greeted as a god by the messengers of Montezuma, and welcomed to the shores of the New World with regal gifts. The Spaniards responded with volleys of gunfire and cannon shots. Never having seen or heard such things before, the Indians were terrified. When they returned to Montezuma to report on their mission, they vividly depicted their first experience with the "blond gods from beyond the sea."

> The sound of the command to fire was very startling. We were deafened by the thunder following the command. A stone ball came out, shooting sparks and raining fire. The smoke that came out smelled like putrid mud. It went right to the head, and made us dizzy. When the ball hit a mountain, it cracked open. If aimed against a tree, the tree shattered into splinters, as if it had exploded from the inside.

Spanish mastiffs were bred and trained for fierceness. Spaniards often amused themselves by encouraging their "pets" to tear unarmed Indians apart and to eat them alive. The cause was more righteous, from the Spanish point of view, if the Indians could be accused of wrongdoing. Here, the unfortunate victims have been accused of practicing sodomy. From de Bry, Historia Americae. *Reproduced from the Collections of the Library of Congress.*

1519

The Spaniards appeared as strange to the Indians as the Indians did to the Spaniards. The Indians found the newcomers odd in appearance and habits, and they were at first mystified by the peculiar-looking animals on which the Europeans sat, and recoiled in horror at the size and ferocity of the Spaniards' hunting dogs. Even Montezuma himself was terrified when his scouts described the awesome spectacle.

> They were armed in iron, with iron on their heads. When they mounted their deer, they were roof-high. Some had black hair, some yellow, and the yellow-haired had yellow beards. They did not eat human hearts. Their dogs were very big, with folded ears, great hanging chops, and fiery, flaming eyes, pale yellow eyes, and yellow bellies. Their tongues hung out, they were always panting, and their hair was flecked like a jaguar's.

Greedy Spaniards tore gold from the Aztec treasures Montezuma had sent them as gifts, and melted it down. From Sahagún, The Florentine Codex, *bk. 12.*

1519

Though the Spanish were believed to be gods when they arrived in Mexico, and presented with some of the rare treasures of Montezuma's kingdom, it was not long before they were displaying a very human avarice. Cortés was not satisfied until he had accumulated a vast storehouse of gold, silver, and precious stones, and, like the Panamanian Indian confronted with the greed of Balboa's men, one Aztec bore eloquent testimony to the spectacle the conquerors made of themselves for the sake of a few ounces of gold:

> When they were given these presents, the Spaniards burst into smiles; their eyes shone with pleasure. . . . They picked up the gold and fingered it like monkeys; they seemed to be transported by joy, as if their hearts were illuminated and made new. . . . Their bodies swelled with greed, and their hunger was ravenous. They hungered like pigs for that gold. They snatched at the golden ensigns, waved them from side to side and examined every inch.

Atahualpa, a Bible in his hand, meets with Francisco Pizarro and Padre Valdeverde in the main square of Cajamarca. From Cristóbal Mena, La Conquista del Peru (Seville, 1534). Rare Books and Manuscripts Division, NYPL.

1533

The Spanish conquistadors served two masters—their sovereign and their pope. In 1493 Pope Alexander VI, in his bull entitled *Inter cetera divina,* had divided the New World between Spain and Portugal. To Charles V of the Holy Roman Empire (who was also Charles I of Spain) went all of South America except Brazil. According to the provisions of this bull, therefore, Peru was the possession of Spain. Padre Valdeverde, the chaplain of Francisco Pizarro's forces, announced this fact to the Inca ruler, Atahualpa, when they met in the main square of Cajamarca.

Valdeverde threatened Atahualpa and his people with death unless he, as their leader, acknowledged his subservience to both Charles V and the pope. Atahualpa was amazed. How could this king and this pope, neither of whom had ever set foot on the soil of Peru, believe that the land was theirs? How could they possibly think it their prerogative to destroy the Incas at will for refusing to accept the rule of the Spanish sovereign and the Christian god? Incredulous about what the Spaniard had told him, Atahualpa threw the Bible on the ground and exclaimed:

> Your emperor may be a great prince: I do not doubt it, seeing that he has sent his subjects so far across the waters; and I am willing to treat him as my brother. As for the pope of whom you speak, he must be mad to speak of giving away countries that do not belong to him. As for my faith, I will not change it. Your own god, as you tell me, was put to death by the very men he created. But my god still looks down upon his children.

Atahualpa's "god" was Pachacamac, or Viracocha, the Incan creator god, who was considered the power behind everything the Incas did. Wishing to emphasize *their* power in terms the Incas would understand, the Spaniards said that they, too, acted according to the wishes of Pachacamac, meaning, of course, the Christian God. The Spanish clearly had superior military strength, and grudgingly, Atahualpa was forced to admit that what they said might be true, and that both Charles V and the pope were acting under the orders of the Incan god. On 20 August he finally submitted to Padre Valdeverde.

Even as he surrendered to his conquerors, and converted to Christianity to avoid a painful death, Atahualpa could not reconcile the Christian message of peace with the unrelenting cruelty of the Spaniards as they cut an ugly path of destruction through the Peruvian provinces through which they passed. Before he was killed he begged them one last time to take pity on his people.

> How is it that you say on the one hand that you have come to talk of friendship and brotherhood and perpetual peace . . . while on the other you have caused so many deaths and such destruction in the provinces you have passed through, without speaking to any of our people to ask if their attitude is friendly or hostile? For, since this was done so completely without provocation on our part against you, I suppose that those two princes [the pope and Charles V] have bidden you to do it, and they must have been bidden by Pachacamac. If this is so, I repeat that you may do whatever you will with me. I only beg you to take pity on my people, for their affliction and death will grieve me more than my own.

Given a choice between death by burning if he remained unbaptized, and death by strangulation if he converted to Christianity, Atahualpa chose death by strangulation. From Garcilaso de la Vega, The Royal Commentaries of Peru (London, 1688). Rare Books and Manuscripts Division, NYPL.

23

1540

Most of the North American Indians lived peacefully in their small communities, subsisting by fishing in the streams, gathering roots and berries, tilling the soil, and hunting the abundant wildlife of their virgin forests and plains. Their world consisted mainly of villages having fewer than a hundred inhabitants.

To the tribes in North America, the arrival of European expeditions, with hundreds of men and animals at one time, must have seemed as devastating as Genghis Khan's invasion to the people of China four centuries earlier. They had never before seen so many people in one place. When Hernando de Soto, proudly proclaiming his lofty position as representative of the Spanish king, arrived at the Creek Indian village of Achese (in what is now Georgia) with six hundred soldiers, Indian prisoners he had taken in Cuba and as he marched through Florida, pigs, horses, and forty mastiffs, he frightened the entire population of the village into a nearby river, where they stayed, cowering in terror. At last the Creek chief was persuaded to leave his hiding place. Despite his fear, he ceremoniously welcomed the Spaniard and his retinue, saying that had he known of de Soto's arrival in advance, he would have been able to prepare a more fitting welcome for him and his men.

> Very high, powerful, and good master. The things that seldom happen bring astonishment. Think, then, what must be the effect, on me and mine, of the sight of you and your people, whom we have at no time seen, astride the fierce brutes, your horses, entering with such speed and fury into my country, that we had no tidings of your coming—things so altogether new, as to strike awe and terror into our hearts, which it was not our nature to resist, so that we should [would be certain to] receive you with the sobriety due to so kingly and famous a lord. Trusting to your greatness and personal qualities, I hope no fault will be found in me, and that I shall rather receive favors, of which one is that with my person, my country, and my vassals, you will do as with your own things; and another, that you will tell me who you are, whence you come, whither you go, and what it is you seek, that I may the better serve you.

Die Indianer greiffen die Spanier an/schlagen ihren Obersten zu todt/ endtlich werden sie doch verjagt. Aber es kommen andere frische Indianer/ die vberfallen vnd vberwinden die Spanier widerumb/ in dem bekommen die Spanier ein Hinderhalt/ vnd welche noch vn verletzt waren auß der Schlacht kommen / dieselbe ziehen darvon.

Indian soldiers, on foot and without armor, attempt to defend themselves against the fully armed Spaniards. From de Bry, Historia Americae. *Reproduced from the Collections of the Library of Congress.*

Relaxing in the home of Don Gonzalo, Girolamo Benzoni discusses with his host the many indignities the Indians have suffered at the hands of the Spaniards. From de Bry, Historia Americae. *Reproduced from the Collections of the Library of Congress.*

1541

The Spaniards enslaved many Indians, and they had an insatiable desire for the products that slave labor brought them. What their workers did was never enough to suit them, and they constantly grumbled that their exhausted, starving vassals were lazy.

Don Gonzalo, a seventy-year-old Nicaraguan Indian who managed to survive his hard lot in life, confided to Girolamo Benzoni, an Italian traveler, his considered opinion of the Spaniards he had known.

> Christians refuse to work. They are cheats, gamblers, depraved, and sacrilegious. When they go to church, they listen intently to the Mass, purge those who don't attend, set traps and inflict injuries on those others. Ultimately, it turns out that one must conclude that Christians are by no means good. And, since I make note of this, doing these things, they are, on the contrary, bad, not good. Where are the good ones? To be sure, I myself have certainly not yet known any good ones, only bad ones.

French Jesuits bring Christianity to Brazil, *From Claude d'Abbeville,* Histoire de la mission des pères capucines . . . *(Paris, 1614). Rare Books and Manuscripts Division, NYPL.*

ca. 1550

When the Portuguese came to Brazil, they cruelly mistreated and enslaved the Indians. And when they had exhausted the adults, they threatened to carry off and make slaves of their children as well.

The Tupinambá Indians of Maranhão, a small island off the northern coast of Brazil, had suffered greatly by the time the French Jesuits arrived there. One of them lamented the sad recent history of his tribe to the French Jesuit Claude d'Abbeville.

> In the beginning the Portuguese did nothing but trade with us, without wishing to live here in any other way. At that time they freely slept with our daughters, which our women . . . considered a great honor. But the Europeans invariably began to insist that the Indians help them build settlements, and fortifications to dominate the surrounding country. And, after having worn out the slaves taken as prisoners of war, they wanted to take our children.

The Indians relish one of their rare opportunities to retaliate against the Spaniards for some of the cruelties they have suffered, as they pour molten gold down the throats of their captives. From de Bry, Historia Americae. *Reproduced from the Collections of the Library of Congress.*

ca. 1550

By the 1550s, many coastal Carib tribes had had first-hand experience with European duplicity. One tribe on the Pacific coast of Darien (now Panama) that had been defrauded by the Spaniards determined to take revenge. Members of the tribe set upon their tormentors, bound them hand and foot, and prepared to kill them. In a last act of exquisite retribution, they melted down the gold that the Spaniards had so coveted, and poured it down the throat of each doomed conquistador in turn, crying:

Eat, eat gold, Christian!

After persuading his cannibal captors to spare his life, Hans Staden is forced to watch them cook another, less fortunate victim. From Theodor de Bry, Grands voyages *(Frankfurt, 1590). Reproduced from the Collections of the Library of Congress.*

1552

The Tupinambás, like many of their neighbors, were friendly toward the French, but despised both the Spanish and the Portuguese. Hans Staden, a young German, was on a Spanish expedition when he was shipwrecked in Tupinambá territory. Knowing the Indians' love of the French, Staden tried to pretend to the tribe (who were cannibals) that he was a Frenchman.

Others before had attempted to fool the Tupinambás by claiming to be French, and the Indians threatened several times to throw Staden into the great communal stew pot if he could not prove he was not Spanish or Portuguese. With considerable ingenuity, Staden each time responded in an invented "language" that sounded different enough from either to convince Konyan Bebe, chief of the tribe, that he belonged to neither of the hated groups. At last, the chief decided to spare Staden's life, but not before he made clear his skepticism about European honesty.

> I have already captured and eaten five Portuguese. They all claim to be French—but they lie!

This woodcut shows the Brazilian Indians hard at work cutting down dyewood. The wood was then shipped to France, which was eager for products from South America. From André Thevet, Les singularitéz de la France antarctique (Paris, 1558). Reproduced from the Collections of the Library of Congress.

1556–58

Living in a land of lush vegetation, the Tupinambás of Guanabara, Brazil, were puzzled by the attitude of the Europeans. They could not understand why anyone who had enough to eat, and was happy and comfortable at home, would leave his native land. Nor could they see why, having enough to satisfy their needs, the Europeans still wanted more—more food, more clothes, more gold and precious stones. One Tupinambá provided the Calvinist missionary Jean de Léry with a vivid and perceptive, if ironic, comparison of the European and Indian lifestyles.

> Why do you people, you French and Portuguese, come from so far away to seek wood to warm you? Don't you have enough wood in your country? . . . You French are great madmen. You cross the sea and suffer great inconvenience, as you say, when you arrive here, and work so hard to accumulate riches for your children or for those who survive you. Is the land that nourished you not sufficient to feed them, too? We have fathers, mothers, and children whom we love. But we are certain that after our death the land that nourished us will also feed them. We therefore rest without further cares.

Many Tupinambá Indians killed themselves and their children rather than submit to slavery under the Portuguese. From Girolamo Benzoni, La Historia del Mondo Nuovo *(Venice, 1572). Rare Books and Manuscripts Division, NYPL.*

ca. 1558

Some of the Tupinambá Indians remained near Bahía (on Brazil's eastern coast) even after the Portuguese came. Others, fiercely protective of their traditions and families, decided that life in the wild rain forests to the north was preferable to the life that would be theirs should they choose to remain in their native villages under Portuguese domination, and some committed suicide rather than submit to the conquerors.

Those who remained made a distinction, however, between the cruel Portuguese colonial authorities and the Portuguese Jesuits, many of whom sympathized with their plight. Reassuring the Portuguese Jesuit José de Anchieta that they bore the Company of Jesus no ill will, they nevertheless insisted on their need to flee from this new wave of invaders, as one of the Tupinambás declared.

> We must go, we must go before these Portuguese arrive. We are not fleeing from the church or from your Company. If you want to go with us, we will live with you deep in the forest or the bush. . . . But these Portuguese will not leave us in peace. You see how a few of them came among us and are seizing our brothers. What could we expect if the rest were to come? They would surely enslave us and our children.

Huejotzingo was an independent province that had never paid tribute to the Aztec empire. The Huejotzingans had welcomed the Spaniards and had even joined with the Tlaxcalans in helping them conquer the powerful Mexicas. And unlike the Panamanians, they did not feel exploited by Cortés. But the habits of independence made them feel they had joined the Spanish as equals—and equal rulers over the Mexicas. They therefore resented the fact that the Spanish gave a larger share of the credit for the conquest, and greater privileges, to the Tlaxcalans, and were shocked when the representative of Philip II levied a crippling tribute assessment on the town. The town council determined that the only way for their people to continue to have enough to eat was for them to take the extraordinary step of appealing directly to the king himself. In desperation, the Indian leader, Don Leonardo Ramirez, and fifteen members of the town council wrote a letter to the Spanish sovereign:

> Catholic Royal Majesty:
> . . . all the while since your subjects the Spaniards arrived, all the while we have been looking toward you, we have been confidently expecting that sometime your pity would reach us . . . no one intimidated us, no one forced us . . . voluntarily we adhered to you, so that we gladly received the newly arrived Spaniards who reached us here in New Spain. For we left our homes behind to go a great distance to meet them; we went twenty leagues to greet Captain General don Hernando Cortés and the others whom he led. We received them gladly, we embraced them, we saluted them with many tears, though we were not acquainted with them . . . Since they are our neighbors, therefore we loved them, nowhere did we attack them. Truly we fed them; some arrived sick so that we carried them in our arms and on our backs, and we served them in many other ways which we are not able to say here . . . all the conquerors know it well . . . we were the only ones who went along while they conquered and made war here in New Spain until they had finished the conquest . . . though some of us were destroyed in it, nor were any of our subjects [e.g., the Mexicas] left . . . We are afflicted, sore pressed, and your town and city of Huejotzingo is as if it is about to disappear and be destroyed. Here is what is being done to us: Now your stewards, the royal officials and the prosecuting attorney Dr. Maldonado are assessing us a very great tribute . . . 14,800 pesos in money, and also all the bushels of maize.
> Our lord sovereign, never has such a thing happened to us in all the time since your servants and vassals the Spaniards came to

The arrival of the Aztec tribute collectors. Photograph by H. S. Rice, courtesy of the American Museum of Natural History.

us, for your servant Don Hernando Cortés, [formerly] Captain General, the Marqués del Valle, in all the time he lived here with us, always greatly cherished us and kept us happy; he never disturbed or agitated us. Although we gave him tribute, he assigned it to us only with moderation; even though we gave him gold, it was only very little—no matter how much, or in what way, or if it was not very pure, he just received it gladly. He never reprimanded us or afflicted us, because it was evident to him and he understood well how very greatly we served and aided him. . . .

Your poor vassals who bow down humbly to you from afar.

Felipe Guzmán Poma de Ayala was the son of an Incan princess and a Spanish aristocrat. Well educated, fluent in Spanish as well as his native language, he traveled throughout Peru talking to the Indians and recording the history and customs of his people. They gave him the information on which he based his book, *The First New Chronicle and Good Government (La primera nueva corónica y buen gobierno)*, originally in the form of a 1,200-page "letter," which he was planning to present to Philip II of Spain. It never reached the king, and was in fact lost for over three centuries. The original manuscript was discovered in the Royal Library of Copenhagen in 1908 but was not published until 1927 (in Spanish). (It was translated into English in 1973.) The book is profusely illustrated by the author, and describes all aspects of Incan life as well as presenting a dynamic picture of the mistreatment of the Incas by the Spanish.

In the course of his travels Guzmán Poma suffered great personal hardship, and considerable humiliation at the hands of the Spanish, who treated him like an outcast wherever he went. He returned home, after many years, poor and unrecognized. In his book, Guamán Poma is understandably bitter about the way in which the Spanish conquerors had treated his countrymen, his family, and himself. He resented physical maltreatment of the Indians, and the deprivation and impoverishment which Spanish rule had brought to Peru. He accused the Spanish of being dishonest in their dealings with the Indians, and wrote:

> It must be realized that the magistrates, mercenaries, priests, and Spaniards in general ill-treated the poor Indian men and women, although the latter were in their own land, and the former were outsiders. The Spaniards did not fear God, nor the justice of His power, when they abused [the Indians] without taking into account [the fact that] the real owners of the country are the Indians.

Felipe Guzmán Poma de Ayala sets out on his thirty-year odyssey through Peru. Here he is accompanied by his son. Note their hispanicized dress. From Ayala, La Primera Nueva corónica y buen gobierno. *(Lima, 1587). Photograph by Logan, courtesy of the American Museum of Natural History.*

This French woodcut shows an Indian fête at Rouen, which was presented for the edification and enjoyment of the court of Charles IX. The "actors" were really Guaraní Indians whose village had been reconstructed to scale for the occasion. From C'est la Deduction de Somptueux Ordre (Paris, 1551). Bibliothèque nationale, Paris.

1562

When they were brought to Europe, Indians from the Spanish and Portuguese colonies usually went in chains. By contrast, those from the French territories were generally well treated. When they were taken to France they were considered honored guests, were presented at court, and gave entertainments for the aristocracy. Many even learned French.

An authentic replica of a Guaraní village was erected to house some of these Indians outside Rouen, where a group of Guaranís was presented to France's twelve-year-old king, Charles IX. The essayist Montaigne had an opportunity to interview them at the time.

Montaigne was eager to know what had most impressed the Indians about the French way of life. There were two things, a Guaraní replied, that he found most extraordinary, strange, and memorable:

> . . . [that] so many big men, strong, armed, and bearded, like those surrounding the king [he was probably referring to the king's guards], should agree to obey a child instead of choosing one of their own group to command them; . . . having seen how half the people had enough comforts and more, while the other half were emaciated by hunger and poverty . . . how the needy half could bear such injustice, nor why they did not seize the others by the throat and burn down their houses. *

* Anticipating by some two centuries what actually happened in France during the French Revolution.

Some of the wanton cruelty that inspired the Indians to revolt against the Spanish. In Florida, Hernando de Soto's party capriciously mutilated and tortured helpless natives for no apparent reason. From de Bry, Historia Americae. *Reproduced from the Collections of the Library of Congress.*

1568

Locked in combat for control of Florida, the Spaniards and the French made full use of their Indian allies. When Captain Dominique de Gourgues arrived in Florida from France in April, he began to plan for the defeat of the Spanish forces.

After suffering brutalization and torment under Spanish rule, the Timucuan Indians, under Saturiba, were eager to dispose of their hated oppressors and at a special council meeting, the powerful chief pledged to the French the allegiance of his tribe in their upcoming war against the detested Spaniards. He told Gourgues that they hadn't had a good day since the Spanish arrived and described how his people had been driven from their homes, their wives and daughters raped, and their children murdered. Gourgues promised that the French would soon punish the Spanish for the evils they had committed. Saturiba, delighted, exclaimed:

> What? Would you really wage war on the Spaniards? What a great good you would be doing us [fighting the Spanish on our behalf]: We [Saturiba and the other Timucuan chiefs] and our subjects will go with you, and will die with you if necessary . . . . Don't worry, we wish them more harm than you do.

2

The 17th Century
Hostages, Slaves, and Allies

By the end of the 16th century, France, Spain, Portugal, and England were attempting to establish colonies in the New World. They made little change in their previous harsh patterns of exploitation and settlement, and the relentless onslaught of European explorers, traders, and armies took its toll on the Indians. They at first welcomed the newcomers, but, as before, saw their hospitality repaid with treachery, and watched in horror as their people died from the effects of war, disease, and persecution.

The papal bull of 1493 allocated Brazil, alone of the countries in the New World, to Portugal, which consequently confined its activities to exploiting that region. Elsewhere, the wave of conquest spread north from South America and Mexico through what is today the southwestern United States and the eastern seaboard. Although the Indians soon realized the advantages of European trade and technology, they sometimes understood too late that with them came the introduction of European ideas and culture that caused schism and demoralization among themselves. Some Indians willingly ceded their lands to the newly arrived Europeans, only to discover that they were destined to pay a devastating price for their generosity.

In 1598, Don Juan de Oñate led several hundred Spanish conquistadors across the Rio Grande from Mexico, taking possession, in the name of the Spanish crown, of the territory (now New Mexico) and its inhabitants. Thus began eighty-two years of Spanish control, during which the Pueblo Indians were forced to submit to the Spanish yoke, become serfs to their conquerors, convert to Christianity, and suffer religious persecution when they tried to keep alive their ancient religious traditions. When their oppressors' strictures became unbearable, Popé, a Pueblo medicine man, organized his hitherto docile tribe to fight back. In 1680 they staged a massive revolt that succeeded in driving the Spaniards back to Mexico and keeping them out of Pueblo lands for the next twelve years despite their superiority of arms.

Spanish hegemony in the New World was challenged by other European nations. The French had been actively exploring since Giovanni da Verrazano's trip in 1524. They had failed in their attempts to settle in established Spanish territories, in Florida, where they were badly beaten by the Spanish in 1565, but in 1603 the ground was laid for the first permanent French colony when Samuel de Champlain led an expedition along the St. Lawrence River. During the 17th century the territory of "New France" gradually spread outward from Quebec, along the St. Lawrence, the Great Lakes, and the Mississippi River as far as the Gulf of Mexico. This expansion was made possible through the efforts of such explorers as René Robert Cavelier (Sieur de La Salle), Father Jacques Marquette, Louis Joliet, Jean Nicolet, Father Louis Hennepin, and government officials like Governor General Louis de Buaude (Comte de Frontenac) and Jean Baptiste Talon, the French intendant at Quebec. In 1607 Sir Walter Raleigh established the first permanent English settlement at Jamestown (now in Virginia), in an area ruled by Powhatan, the powerful chief of an Algonquian-speaking confederacy whose borders stretched from the Potomac River almost as far south as Albemarle Sound in North Carolina.

European rivalries in the New World echoed the political and military battles in the Old, and the conquerors tried to impose the same absolute control over the Indians that they wanted over their conquered European enemies. But relations between the Indians and settlers in what is today the United States were different from what they had been between the Spaniards and the Aztecs and the various tribes in South America only a century earlier. Some northerly tribes were bickering among themselves and were weaker than their southerly brothers when the Europeans arrived, and sought alliances with the newcomers to "protect" themselves. Powhatan and Captain John Smith cooperated with each other, thus helping the settlers to adjust to a difficult life in a strange land. Later, and farther north Indian tribes in Maryland sold their land to the newcomers and moved south of the Potomac River.

Unlike the Spaniards, the English were seeking neither gold nor slaves; rather they wanted to tame their new and frequently hostile environment. They needed the Indians' knowledge to help them survive and learn how to exploit their surroundings for their own advantage. Nevertheless, frequent misunderstandings, and even armed conflicts, arose, often as a result of the colonists' greed, as they sought to take possession of more and more land, to control the Indians who lived on it, and to establish permanent settlements. The Indians sometimes realized that, despite treaties and other agreements, the settlers were defrauding them in an attempt to turn them into subject peoples.

When he was offered a crown by the English in 1609, Powhatan refused to go to Jamestown to receive it, insisting instead that the English come to him. Captains Christopher Newport and John Smith finally went to Powhatan's capital at Weremoco (now Gloucester County, Virginia) for the ceremony. There, the chieftain accepted both the crown and the other gifts offered to him, but absolutely refused to kneel in homage to the king of England. According to Indian tradition, he reciprocated with gifts of his own—his old shoes and his mantle. Certainly not the munificent gifts an important vassal was expected to send to his omnipotent lord!

This incident precipitated a period of strained relations, and in 1622 Powhatan's aging brother and successor, Opechancanough, led a raiding party that destroyed several settlements and killed 350 colonists. Allying themselves with hostile Indians converted to Christianity, the whites retaliated. By the time the bloodshed was over in 1644, they had killed Opechancanough and crushed the once-powerful Algonquin confederacy.

Farther north, in New York, New Jersey, and Pennsylvania, there developed a similar pattern of exploitation, callousness, and subjugation by fiat. In the most famous of many similar arrangements, in 1624 the Indians in New York were induced to sell Manhattan Island to the Dutch for the equivalent of $24.00. Seventeen years later the Dutch cruelly massacred some Wappinger Indians who had run to them for protection against marauding Mohawks. In 1696, Onondaga and Oneida fortified villages were burned to the ground by the French, and the cornfields surrounding the Mohawk settlement in New York were also destroyed. The Dutch and the Swedes "bought" an extensive tract of land in New Jersey and eastern Pennsylvania for a pittance from the Delawares—they offered a pot of brandy for land worth, at the end of the century, over £400 in Pennsylvania currency. Also in "friendly" Pennsylvania (because of the Indians' relationship with William Penn, it had a reputation for fair dealing), one group of Delawares was persuaded to exchange 700 acres of land for some liquor, two coats, two axes, two barrels of lard, four handfuls of powder, and two knives. The English quite often simply seized what they wanted, claiming they owned all of North America by right of prior discovery and that no one— including the Indians—could claim ownership of land except by a grant from the English king. And counterfeit wampum was made in New Jersey and Long Island, thus effectively undermining the Indians' use of it as a staple monetary base in those areas.

In New England, Massasoit, chief of the Wampanoags, negotiated a treaty with the Pilgrims that lasted from 1621 until he died forty years later. There followed sporadic violence, after which the chief's son Metacom (called King Philip by the English) organized a temporarily successful attempt to drive out the white men. For a year, he held his own, but in 1676 his food ran out, and an Indian informer betrayed him. Metacom was captured. His wife, his nine-year-old son, and many other members of his band were sold into slavery, but before they could be shipped to the West Indies to begin their servitude, the English killed and quartered Metacom and displayed his severed head on a pole in the public square.

The French were by now firmly entrenched in Canada, where the Jesuits systematically converted the Indians to Christianity and tried to teach them to speak, dress, and act like Frenchmen. The Huron Indians of the St. Lawrence Valley cooperated with Samuel de Champlain, who built a powerful system of fortifications from which he terrorized the Onondagas and in 1609 seized their villages. In so doing, he earned the enmity of the mighty Iroquois Confederacy (also known as the League of the Iroquois, or the League of the Five Nations), with which the Onondagas were allied. These five affiliated tribes (Senecas, Onondagas, Mohawks, Cayugas, and Oneidas) then united with the British against the French, helping eventually to drive the latter out of their North American colonies. In the general peacemaking at Albany, an extensive Indian-white confederation called the Covenant Chain was created under the aegis of the colony of New York. It linked a number of English colonies, with New York as their spearhead, with an alliance of Indian tribes, with the Iroquois as their leader. Each European power in this region in turn used its Indian allies, urging them to fight against its foes. In this way, both the English and the French exploited existing intertribal rivalries.

Groups of Indians were presented at the English court, as they had been at the French. Among these Indians was Pocahontas, who was renamed "The Lady Rebecca" by the English after her marriage to John Rolfe and conversion to Christianity, in deference to the status of her father, Chief Powhatan. (She was considered to be the daughter of a king.)

Some Indian girls were shipped to Bermuda to learn how to behave like Christian ladies, so that they could return to convert their tribes, but their lot was better than most. Large numbers of Indians from the Carolinas were enslaved and carried off to Bermuda, Barbados, and Jamaica. Governor Joseph West of South Carolina lined his pockets with the profits from this enterprise, and even induced Indians to capture other Indians so that their sale could add to his coffers. The situation deteriorated until, in 1693, the Cherokees urgently petitioned Thomas Smith, who was then governor of the South Carolina territory, to save them from the Catawbas, Shawnees, and Congarees, who had themselves been selling them profitably as slaves both to local planters and for shipment outside the country. But nothing was done to solve the problem permanently.

European opinion was still divided on how to treat the Indians. Although many Europeans continued to exploit the New World's first inhabitants, they could not always do so with impunity. When Jacques de Denonville captured twenty-one Indians and took them to France "dressed in gorgeous French garments," as one eyewitness reported, other influential noblemen found this abduction so odious that when Louis de Frontenac succeeded Denonville as the governor of New France in 1689, they forced the "conqueror" to return these Indians to their native Canada. Despite this demonstration of sympathy for the Indians, Louis XIV continued to order Indian slaves to serve on his royal galleys. And so it went for the Indians, as capricious rulers in Europe alternated sympathy with exploitation in their dealings with them throughout the century.

Samuel de Champlain, who attempted to convert many Indians in Canada to Christianity, helped the Algonquins defeat the Iroquois at Fort Ticonderoga in 1609. Killing the Iroquois chief with a shot from his arquebus, Champlain earned the lasting enmity of the tribe, who sided with the British in future conflicts. From Champlain, Les Voyages . . . *(Paris, 1633). Reproduced from the Collections of the Library of Congress.*

1603

Invited to stay with the friendly Hurons at St. Matthew's Point in Quebec, near Tadoussac on the St. Lawrence River, Samuel de Champlain and Father Joseph Le Carron held many discussions with them, pointing out the superiority of Christianity and the French way of life. The Indians listened attentively but demanded proof before they would agree to change their own ways, and the two Frenchmen were amazed at the comment made by Anadabijou, chief of the Hurons.

> You say things that pass our knowledge, and which we cannot understand by words, being beyond our comprehension; but if you would do us a service, come and dwell in this country, bringing your wives and children, and when they are here we shall see how you serve the God you worship, and how you live with your wives and children, how you cultivate and plant the soil, how you obey your laws, how you take care of animals, and how you manufacture all that we see proceeding from your inventive skill. When we see all this, we shall learn more in a year than in twenty by simply hearing you discourse; and if we cannot then understand, you shall take our children, who shall be as your own. And thus being convinced that our life is a miserable one in comparison with yours, it is easy to believe that we shall adopt yours, abandoning our own.

This pencil drawing shows Captain John Smith crowning Powhatan at Weremoco.
Smithsonian Institution, National Anthropological Archives.

1609

When his supplies ran short, Captain John Smith made extensive trips up the Chicahominy River in the colony of Virginia to try to trade with the Algonquins for corn. In the course of one of these journeys he was ambushed and captured by some of the tribe and brought to Weremoco on the York River (now Gloucester County, Virginia). There Powhatan (Pau't-hanne, "Falls in a Current," "Hill of the Powwow"), also known as Wahunsonacock, chief of the Algonquin Confederacy, made a speech to Smith in which he sharply criticized the excessive force and cruelty used by the British in their efforts to subjugate his people (though he and Smith later became close friends).

> I will spare you what I can, and that within two days. But Captain Smith, I have some doubts as to your object in this visit. I am informed that you wish to conquer more than to trade, and at all events you know my people must be afraid to come near you with their corn, so long as you go armed and with such a retinue. Lay aside your weapons, then. Here they are needless. We are all friends, all Powhatans [members of the Powhatan confederacy].
>
> Captain Smith, I have seen two generations of my people die. Not a man of the two generations is alive now but myself. I am now old, and must die soon. My authority must descend to my brothers Opitchapan, Opechancanough, and Catatough—then to my two daughters. I wish them to know as much as I do and

43

that you love them as I do. I wish to live quietly with you, and I wish the same for my successors. Now the rumors that reach me on all hands make me uneasy. What do you expect to gain by destroying us who provide you with food? And what can you get by war, if we escape you and hide our provisions in the woods? We are unarmed too, you see. Do you believe me such a fool as not to prefer eating good meat, sleeping quietly with my wives and children, laughing and making merry with you, having copper and hatchets and anything else—as your friend—to flying from you as your enemy, lying cold in the woods, eating acorns and roots, and being so hunted by you meanwhile, that if but a twig break, my men will cry out, "Here comes Captain Smith!" Let us be friends, then. Do not invade us thus with such an armed force. Lay aside these arms.

Champlain faced constant danger of attack from hostile Indians, though he was protected by those friendly to him. Here Indians are attacking the French on land and from boats, and burning them alive. From Champlain, Les Voyages. Reproduced from the Collections of the Library of Congress.

1613

Tessouat (called Le Borgne, or "Blind in One Eye," by the French because of his infirmity), chief of the Ottawas, was outspoken in his denunciations of the treachery of Frenchmen toward each other. Learning that Champlain had been forced to undergo needless hardship in attempting to explore regions which Nicolas de Vignau had falsely described in a letter, Tessouat roundly berated de Vignau in Champlain's presence.

> You are a liar. You know very well you slept here among my children every night, and got up again every morning; and if you ever went to the Nipissings, it must have been when you were asleep. How can you be so imprudent as to lie to your chief, and so wicked as to risk his life among so many dangers? We ought to kill you with tortures worse than those with which we kill our enemies. You are a liar. Which way did you go? By what lakes? Who went with you? [Then, turning to Champlain, Tessouat added:] Give him to us and we promise you he shall never lie again.

Three converted Tupinambá Indians brought to perform at the court of Louis XIII. Shown here in the dancing costumes they wore for the occasion, they present an interesting picture of different styles, the typical French court dress and crucifixes contrasting with their own traditional headdresses and musical instruments. From Yves d'Évreux, Suite de l'histoire . . . 1613 et 1614 *(Paris, 1615). Rare Books and Manuscripts Division, NYPL.*

1613–14

In their zeal to convert the Tupinambá Indians of Brazil to Christianity, the French frequently glamorized the advantages of the European way of life and denigrated the traditional Tupinambá culture. On one of these occasions, Chief Iacoupen of the Tupinambás berated the Capuchin monk Yves d'Evreux for being illogical.

> I observe that the French abound in riches, are valorous, have invented ships that cross the seas, cannon and powder to kill men invisibly, are well dressed and fed, and are feared and respected. We, on the contrary, have remained errant vagabonds, without axes, scythes, knives, or other tools. What is the reason for this? Two infants are born at the same moment, one French, and the other Tupinambá, both weak and feeble. Yet one is born to have all these commodities, and the other to spend his life poorly. . . . I cannot satisfy my mind when I ponder why you French have knowledge of God rather than we. . . . You tell us that God sent you. Why did he not send you sooner? Our fathers would not have been lost, as [you say] they were. The missionary Fathers are men like us. Why are *they* rather than other men privileged to speak to God?

Ætatis suæ 21. Aº. 1616.

Matoaks als Rebecka daughter to the mighty Prince
Powhatan Emperour of Attanoughkomouck als Virginia
converted and baptized in the Chriſtian faith, and
Wife to the Worll Mr Tho: Rolff.

Pocahontas died in England at the age of 22, shortly after this portrait was painted.
Smithsonian Institution, National Anthropological Archives.

1617

In 1614 Pocahontas (or Matoaka) married John Rolfe, an English colonist, and in 1616 she sailed to England with her husband and her brother-in-law Tomocomo (also known as Uttamatómakkin). Arriving in London, she was surprised to meet Captain John Smith, who had returned home in 1609, as he was reported to have died after an accident.

She was also shocked when he forbade her to call him "father," as she had in Virginia, where he had been treated with respect and affection and considered by Powhatan to be a member of the family. Smith explained to

47

her that the familiarity was forbidden in England, as she was considered a princess and he was not of noble birth.

Pocahontas said this was inconsistent, because their relationship had not changed. At the same time, she reminded him that because her father doubted the figures about the population of England he had been given by the English in Virginia, he had sent Tomocomo to check at first hand.

> Were you not afraid to come into my father's country? Did you not cause fear in him, and all his people [but me]? And fear you here I should call you father? I tell you then, I will, and you shall call me child, and so I will be forever and ever your countryman. They did tell us always [that] you were dead, and I knew no other till I came to Plymouth. Yet Powhatan did command Uttamató-makkin to seek you, and know the truth, because your country-men will lie much.

Indians established amicable trading relations with the English in a number of colonies, but were unwilling to accept English law and the punishments it demanded in place of their own. From de Bry, Historia Americae (1634).
Reproduced from the Collections of the Library of Congress.

1635

In an attempt to subjugate the Algonkin Indians in Maryland, Governor Leonard Calvert demanded that any Indian who killed an Englishman should surrender himself for punishment under English law. After carefully reflecting on this request, the wicomesse (chief) rejected it, saying that the imposition of foreign law was unacceptable to his people.

> It is the manner among us Indians, that if any such accident should happen, we redeem the life of a man who is killed in that way with 100 arm's length of roanoke [a form of wampum beads used as money]. Since you are strangers here, you should rather conform to the customs of our country, than impose yours upon us.

When the Mohegans defeated the Narragansetts in 1643, the Mohegan chief Uncas turned Miantonomo over to the English, who accused him of treachery and sentenced him to death. Uncas was meant to carry out the sentence, but Miantonomo was in fact murdered by Uncas's brother Wawequa. Courtesy of the American Museum of Natural History.

1642

Miantonomo (or Miantonomi, "He Wages War"), a Narragansett chief, pleaded with Waindance, up to that time an enemy, at Meaticut, Long Island, to put aside personal animosity and join with him in a mutual effort to repulse the English, their common foe. (The English were later instrumental in causing Miantonomo's murder.) While excoriating the English for what they had done to the Indians, he nevertheless recommended that the Indians adopt English strategy in order to defeat them.

> Brothers, we must be as one as the English are, or we shall all be destroyed. You know our fathers had plenty of deer and skins and our plains were full of game and turkeys, and our coves and rivers were full of fish.
>
> But, brothers, since these Englishmen have seized our country, they have cut down the grass with scythes, and the trees with axes. Their cows and horses eat up the grass, and their hogs spoil our bed of clams; and finally we shall all starve to death; therefore, stand not in your own light, I ask you, but resolve to act like men. All the sachems [chiefs] both to the east and the west have joined with us, and we are resolved to fall upon them [the English] at a day appointed, and therefore I come secretly to you, because you can persuade your Indians to do what you will.

49

The massacre of Jamestown in 1622, pictured here, was led by Opechancanough and was the beginning of the chief's long campaign to repulse the English, which was ended only by his death. From de Bry, Grands voyages *(1634). Reproduced from the Collections of the Library of Congress.*

1644

After attacking the settlers along the York and Pamunkey rivers, Opechancanough was finally captured by the English in April. Because of his advanced age, he was carried on a litter to Jamestown, where he was imprisoned. On the way, a guard deliberately shot him, inflicting a wound from which he later died. The aged chief sent for Governor William Berkeley, who was then in charge of the Virginia settlement. Then, just before he died, Opechancanough drew himself up on his litter and glared menacingly at the English who were gathered around him. Pointing to the governor, he firmly denounced the English for their lack of respect and their inhumanity:

> If it had been my fortune to take Sir William Berkeley prisoner, I would not have meanly exposed him as a show to my people.

A 17th-century Huron warrior. He is wearing decorated bark clothing and moccasins. From François de Creux, Historiae Canadensis (1664), pt. III, p. 70. Rare Books and Manuscripts Division, NYPL.

1644

Charles de Montmagny, the governor of New France, went to Trois Rivières in an effort to ransom some prisoners being held there by the Hurons. When the Indians rejected his offer of merchandise in exchange for their prisoners, demanding that the French give them the prisoners *they* held instead, he asked them to explain their reasons for insisting on this exchange. Two of the Hurons rejected his invitation to speak, saying that they were warriors and not orators. However, the third Huron, a Christian, addressing the governor as *Onnonthio* (Great Mountain), the Huron translation of Montmagny, explained their reasons fully:

Onnonthio, don't be angry with us because of my brother's speech. If we couldn't decide to give you our prisoners, it is because we have reasons that you will not disapprove of. We would lose honor if we did it, you don't see any old men among us; young men and warriors would be dishonored if instead of returning home with captives they appeared with merchandise. Even you, my Father, what would you say to your soldiers if you saw them come back from war with a load of merchandise? The only desire that you make apparent in having our slaves could be to hold them for ransom; isn't that so? But it is not for us to ignore this. Our brothers the Algonquins have not been able to do what you wanted them to, because they are old men who have no one to answer to for their conduct; being no longer controlled by the same motives as we, they would not have been able honestly to refuse you a thing of such little consequence. Our old people [tribal elders] when they will learn your intentions, will doubtless interpret them in the same way. We all want peace, we share your views, we have even anticipated them, for we have done no harm to our prisoners; we have treated them as soon becoming our friends; but it isn't suitable for us to anticipate the agreement of our old people, nor to deprive them of such a good occasion to show our Father how they respect his wishes.

Another reason holds us back, and I am sure it will not seem less legitimate than the first. We know that the river is covered with our enemies; if we meet any, who are stronger than we, of what use will your gifts be, but to load us down, and inspire them even more to fight, in order to profit from our possessions? But if they see among us some of their brothers, who show them that we want peace, that Onnonthio wants to be the father of all the nations, that he can no longer stand it that his children, whom he loves equally, continue to tear each other apart, the arms will fall from their hands, our prisoners will save our lives and they will work much more effectively toward peace than if we gave them back their liberty too hurriedly.

In spite of the Indians' repeated appeals, no attempt was made by the colonists to curb the sale of liquor. From John Frost, Pictorial History of America *(Auburn, N.Y., 1851).*

1656

Aware of their potential strength as allies of the Dutch, the Mohawk Indians pleaded with them for better treatment. Specifically, they asked Dutch officials to stop the sale of the brandy the Indians knew was sapping their strength and destroying their lives—to "put the bung in their casks." They knew, however, that many Dutch traders would continue to sell brandy outside their territory to any Indian who would buy it.

> When we go away now, we shall take with us a good deal of brandy and after that no more, for we will burn our kegs. However, although we propose that now, it will not be carried out. Therefore, when other Indians come into the country with brandy, we shall come to the Dutch officials and tell them who has sold the brandy to the Indians.

It was after many attacks such as the one pictured here that Passaconaway advised his people to stop trying to keep the English out of their territory. Photograph by J. Kirschner, courtesy of the American Museum of Natural History.

1660

Shortly before his death, Passaconaway, a Narragansett sachem, called his people together to make his farewell speech, according to their custom. He warned his people of the dangers they would still have to face when he was gone, and of the futility of attempting to wage war against the English, advice which was later carefully followed by his son Wonnalancet.

> I am now going the way of all flesh, and am ready to die. I am not likely to see you all together any more. I will now have this word of counsel with you, so that you may be careful how you quarrel with the English. Although you may do them much harm, yet assuredly you will all be destroyed and rooted off the earth if you do. I was as much an enemy of the English as anyone, and tried all possible ways and means to destroy them, or at least to prevent them from settling down here, but I could in no way bring it about. Therefore I advise you never to contend with the English, nor to war against them.

Jacques Cartier, a French navigator who brought Christianity to Canada in the 16th century, watches while a cross is set up at Gaspé. The friendly relations he established were perpetuated by his successors, yet, as we can see from the statement by the Micmacs, the Indians did not hesitate to criticize the French. An engraving from Harper's New Monthly Magazine *(March 1883). Courtesy of The New-York Historical Society, New York City.*

1676

Some French captains in Nova Scotia criticized the Indians, extolling the marvels of French civilization. A Gaspesian (now Micmac) Indian chief living in the area then denigrated the French in his turn:

You reproach us very inappropriately that our country is a little hell on earth in contrast with France, which you compare to a terrestrial paradise, in that it yields you, so you say, every kind of provision in abundance. You say of us also that we are the most miserable and unhappy of all men, living without religion, without manners, without honor, without social order, and in a word, without any rules, like the beasts in our woods and forests, lacking bread, wine, and a thousand other comforts which you have in superfluity in Europe. Well, my brother, if you do not yet know the real feelings which our Indians have toward your country and toward all your nation, it is proper that I inform you at once.

I beg you now to believe that, all miserable as we seem in your eyes, we consider ourselves nevertheless much happier than you, in that we are very content with the little that we have. . . . You deceive yourselves greatly if you think that you can persuade us that your country is better than ours. For if France, as you say, is a little terrestrial paradise, are you wise to leave it? And why abandon wives, children, relatives, and friends? Why risk your life and your property every year? And why expose yourself in all seasons to the storms and tempests of the sea in order to come to a strange and barbarous country which you consider the poorest and least fortunate in the world? Besides, since we are wholly convinced of the contrary, we scarcely take the trouble to go to France because we fear with good reason that we will find little satisfaction there, since we see in our own experience that those who are natives of it leave it every year in order to enrich themselves on our shores. We believe, further, that you are also incomparably poorer than we, and that you are only simply journeymen, valets, servants, and slaves, all masters and grand captains that you may appear, seeing that you glory in our old rags, and in our miserable suits of beaver which can no longer be of use to us and that, by fishing for cod here, you find the means of relieving the misery and the poverty which oppress you. As for us, we find all our riches and all our conveniences among ourselves, without trouble, without exposing our lives to the dangers in which you find yourselves constantly through your long voyages. And while feeling compassion for you in the sweetness of our repose, we wonder at the anxieties and cares which you give yourselves, night and day, in order to load your ships. We see also that all your people live, as a rule, only upon the cod which you catch among us. It is everlastingly nothing but cod—cod in the morning, cod at midday, cod in the evening, and always cod, until things come to such a pass that if you wish some good morsels it is at our expense; and you are obliged to have recourse to the Indians, whom you despise so much, and to beg them to go hunting so that you may eat good food. Now tell me this one little thing, if you have any sense. Which of these two is the wisest and happiest: he who labors without ceasing and obtains only with great trouble enough to live on, or he who rests in comfort and finds all that he needs in the pleasure of hunting and fishing?

It is true that we have not always had the use of bread and wine which your France produces; but, in fact, before the arrival of the French in these parts, did not the Gaspesians live much longer than now? And if we have not any longer among us any of those old men of a hundred and thirty to forty years, it is only because we are gradually adopting your manner of living, for experience is making it very plain that those of us live longest who, despising your bread, your wine, and your brandy, are content with their natural food of beaver, of moose, of waterfowl, and of fish, in accordance with the custom of our ancestors and of all the Gaspesian nation. Learn now, my brother, once for all, because I must open my heart to you: There is no Indian who does not consider himself infinitely more happy and more powerful than the French.

Trading between Delawares and Swedes in the 17th century. From Tomas Campanius Holm, Kort Beskrifning . . . (Stockholm, 1702). Rare Books and Manuscripts Division, NYPL.

1676

When the English criticized the drunken and disorderly behavior of the Delawares of New Jersey, their chief, Okanikon, forcefully put the blame where it rightfully belonged:

> The strong liquor was first sold to us by the Dutch, and they were blind, they had no eyes, they could not see it was for our hurt; the next people that came were the Swedes, who continued the sale of strong liquor to us, we love it so we cannot refuse it, it makes us wild; we do not know what we are doing; we abuse one another; we throw one another into the fire. . . . Through drinking, seven score of our people have been killed.
>
> The cask must be sealed, it must be made fast. It must not leak by day or night, in the light, or in the dark.

PORTRAIT & Signature
of TAMMANY or
TAM-MAN-END
the great Chief of
the DELAWARES.
this Signature was
attached to the Deed of purchase of
Land in 1683 now embraced in Bucks
County Pennsylvania.

(a) Portrait and signature of Tammanend, which was appended to a later agreement with the English. Courtesy of The New-York Historical Society, New York City.

1682

The agreement reached under an elm tree at Shakamaxon (now in Pennsylvania) by Delaware chief Tammany (Tammanend) and William Penn—called by Voltaire "the only treaty never sworn to and never broken"—remained in force until Penn's death. Both the Quaker's pledge and the reply of Tammany have never been equaled for the sincerity of their promises of brotherhood and mutual understanding. Penn said to the assembled Indians:

> We meet on the broad pathway of good faith and good will; no advantage shall be taken on either side, but all shall be openness and love. We are the same as if one man's body was to be divided into two parts; we are of one flesh and blood.

To which Tammany replied:

> We will live in love with William Penn and his children as long as the creeks and rivers run, and while the sun, moon, and stars endure.

The Great God who is the power and wisdom that made you and me Incline your hearts to Righteousness Love and peace. This I send to Assure you of my Love, and to desire your Love to my ffriends, and when the Great God brings me among you I Intend to order all things in such manner that we may all live in Love and peace one with another which I hope the Great God will Incline both me and you to do. I seek nothing but the honor of his name, and that we who are his workmanship, may do that which is well pleasing to him. The man which delivers this unto you, is my special ffriend sober wise and Loving, you may believe him. I have already taken care that none of my people wrong you, by good Laws I have provided for that purpose, nor will I ever allow any of my people to sell Rumm to make your people drunk. If anything should be out of order, expect when I come, it shall be mended, and I will bring you some things of our Country that are useful and pleasing to you. So I rest In y Love of our god that made us

England 25 : 2 : 1682   I am

your Loveing Freind

I writ this to the Indians
by an Interpreter the
6 mo 1682 Tho. Holme

Wm Penn

(b) The reverse side of the treaty between William Penn and the Delawares signed at Shakamaxon. Reproduced from the Collections of the Library of Congress.

59

An Iroquois council meeting much like the one described below, at which a wampum belt is being interpreted. An enlargement of the belt is shown at the center of the picture. From J. F. Lafitau, Moeurs des sauvages . . . *(Paris, 1724).* Rare Books and Manuscripts Division, NYPL.

1684

The English and the Indians held a major council meeting in Albany that was presided over by Lord Howard of Effingham, governor of Virginia, and Colonel Thomas Dongan, governor of New York, and attended by Governor General Joseph Antoine Le Febvre de la Barre of Canada and by representatives of the Five Nations. The Indians asked for protection against the French, and the Onondagas and Cayugas, particularly, reaffirmed their allegiance to the English, asking that the latter treat them as well, now that they were in need of help, as they had treated the English on their arrival in America.

Brother Corlaer,
Your sachem is a great sachem and we are but a small people. When the English came to Manhattan, that is New York, [to] Aragiske, which is now called Virginia, and to Jaquokranogare, now called Maryland, they were but a small people and we a great people, and finding they were good people we gave them land and treated them civilly. And now that you are a great people

and we but a small, you will protect us from the French. If you do not, we shall lose all our hunting and beavers, the French will have all the beavers, and be angry with us for bringing any to you.

Brethren, we have put all our land and ourselves under the protection of the great Duke of York, the brother of your great sachem. We have given the Susquehanna River, which we won with the sword, to this government and desire that it may be a branch of that great tree that grows here, * whose top reaches to the sun, under whose branches we shall shelter ourselves from the French or any other people, and our fire burn in your houses and your fire burn with us. We desire that it always may be so, and do not want any of [William] Penn's people to settle upon the Susquehanna River; for all our folks [and] soldiers are like wolves in the woods, as you, sachem of Virginia, know, since we have no other land to leave to our wives and children.

We have put ourselves under the great sachem Charles [the king] who lives over the great lake [the Atlantic Ocean], and we give you two white dressed deerskins to be sent to the great sachem Charles so that he may write upon them, and put a great red seal on them [acknowledging] that we put [that part of] the Susquehanna River above the Washinta [or] falls and all the rest of our land under the Great Duke of York and nobody else. Our brethren his servants were as fathers to our wives and children, and gave us bread when we were in need of it, and we will neither join ourselves nor our land to any other government than this. And this proposition we desire that Corlaer, the governor, may send over to your great sachem Charles who dwells over the great lake with this belt of *wampumpeag* [white wampum], and another smaller belt for the Duke of York his brother, and we give a beaver to Corlaer to [so he will] send over this proposition.

And you, great man of Virginia, meaning Lord Effingham, governor of Virginia, we let you know that great Penn did speak to us here in Corlaer's house through his agents, and desired to buy the Susquehanna River, but we would not hearken to him or come under his government, and therefore desire you to be witness of what we do now and that we have already done and let your friend who lives over the great lake know that we are a free people uniting ourselves to what [ever] sachem we please, and do give you one beaver skin.

*The Tree of Peace, symbol of unity under the League of the Five Nations.

Frequently, Seneca Indians carrying canoe-loads of beaver skins to be traded, as seen here, were attacked, and their skins seized, by Indians, such as the Miamis, who had been armed by the French. Until they were aided by the British, the Senecas had no ammunition with which to protect themselves. Photograph by H. S. Rice, courtesy of the American Museum of Natural History.

1684

At the same council meeting, Governor de la Barre defended his actions, saying that the Senecas had been using arms supplied by the British against the French, and that he would be forced to retaliate if they persisted. On 5 August, the Senecas replied to the charge, accusing the French of causing the problem themselves, and of acting in bad faith:

> We were sent for, and have come, and have heard what you have said to us, that Corlaer [Iroquois term for the governor of New York] has [had] great complaints about us, both from Virginia and Canada. What they complain of from Canada may possibly be true, that our young people have taken some of their goods; but Onnonthio* is the cause of it. He not only permits his people to carry ammunition, guns, powder, lead, and axes to the Tuituihronoon [Miamis] our enemies, but sends them thither on purpose. These guns which he sends knock our beaver hunters on the head, and our enemies carry the beavers to Canada that we would have brought to our brethren. Our beaver hunters are soldiers, and could bear this no longer. On their way to our enemies (the Miamis), and very near them, they met with some French, carrying ammunition, which our men took from them. This is agreeable to our customs of war, and we may therefore

openly own it; though we know not whether it be practiced by the Christians in similar cases.

When the governor of Canada speaks to us of the chain [i.e., a covenant chain or league of friendship], he calls us children, and says, "I am your father, you must hold fast [to] the chain, and I will do the same. I will protect you as a father does his children." Is this protection, to speak thus with his lips, and at the same time to knock us on the head by assisting our enemies with ammunition?

He always says, "I am your father, and you are my children," and yet he is angry with his children for taking these goods. But, O! Corlaer! O Assarigoa [a term for the governor of Virginia]! We must complain to you. You, Corlaer, are a lord, and govern this country. Is it just that our father is going to fight with us for these things, or is it well done? We rejoiced when La Sal [Robert Cavelier, Sieur de La Salle] was sent over the great water, and when Perot [Nicolas Perrot, a *coureur de bois*, or French trapper] was removed, because they had furnished our enemies with ammunition; but we are disappointed in our hopes, for we find that our enemies are still supplied. Is this well done? Yea, he often forbids us to make war on any of the nations with whom he trades, and at the same time furnishes them with all sorts of ammunition, to enable them to destroy us.

Thus far in answer to the complaints which the governor of Canada has made of us to Corlaer. Corlaer said to us that satisfaction must be made to the French, for the mischief we have done them. This he said before he heard our answer. Now, let him who has inspection over all our countries, on whom our eyes are fixed, let him, Corlaer, judge and determine. If you said it must be paid, we shall pay it, but we cannot live without free beaver hunting.

Corlaer, hear what we say. We thank you for the Duke's [coat of] arms which you have given us to put on our castles [the English term for fortified Iroquois towns along the borders of the colonies], as a defense to [protection for] them. You command them. Have we wandered out of the way [gone astray] as the governor of Canada says? We do not threaten him with war, as he threatens us. What shall we do? Shall we run away, or shall we sit still in our houses? What shall we do? We speak to him that governs and commands us.

Now, Corlaer and Assarigoa, and all people here present, remember what we have answered to the complaints of the governor of Canada. Yea, let what we say come to his ears.

*The term originated as a translation of Montmagny, an earlier governor general of Canada, and came to apply generally to the office.

A schematic representation of Grangula addressing the assembled French officers and the Five Nations at the camp of Governor de la Barre at La Famine. From William M. Beauchamp, A History of the New York Iroquois (Albany, N.Y., 1905). Reproduced from the Collections of the Library of Congress.

1684

At a council meeting held at La Famine (now Salmon, New York), Canada's Governor de la Barre accused the Five Nations of breaking the peace and demanded indemnification for French losses. Grangula (called by the French Grand'Gueule, "Big Mouth"), a famous Onondaga warrior, rose and walked slowly around the circle of French and Indians. Looking squarely at the governor, who was seated in an armchair, the aged orator demonstrated how clearly the Five Nations recognized the treachery and inconsistency of the French, and their inability to carry out their threats.

> Onnonthio, I honor you, and all the warriors who accompany me do the same. Your interpreter has made an end of his discourse, and now I come to begin mine. My voice glides to your ear. Pray listen to my words.
>
> Onnonthio, in setting out from Quebec, you must have imagined that the scorching beams of the sun had burnt down the forests which render our country inaccessible to the French, or else that the inundations of the lake had surrounded our cottages, and confined us prisoners. . . . I must tell you, Onnonthio, I am not asleep, my eyes are open; and the sun that vouchsafes the light gives me a clear view of a great captain at the head of a troop of soldiers, who speaks as if he were asleep. He

pretends that he does not approach this lake with any other view than to smoke with the Onondagas the great calumet [peace pipe]; but the Grangula knows better things, he sees plainly that the Onnonthio meant to knock them on the head, if the French arms had not been so weak.

I perceive that the Onnonthio raves in a camp of sick people, whose lives the Great Spirit has saved [from fighting] by visiting them with infirmities.

You must know, Onnonthio, that we have robbed no French-men except those who supplied the Illinois and the Miamis (our enemies) with guns, with powder, and with ball: These indeed we took care of, because such arms might have cost us our life. Our conduct in that point is of a piece with that of the Jesuits, who stave all the barrels of brandy that are brought to our cantons [districts], lest the people getting drunk should knock them in the head.

We have conducted the English to our lakes, in order to traffic with the Ottawas and the Hurons; just as the Algonquins conducted the French to our five cantons, in order to carry on a commerce that the English lay claim [to] as their right. We are born free men, and have no dependence either upon the Onnonthio or the Corlaer. We have a power to go where we please, to conduct who we will to the places we resort to, and to buy and sell where we think fit. If your allies are your slaves or children, you may even treat them as such, and rob them of the liberty of entertaining any other nation but your own. . . .

We have done less than the English and the French, who, without any right, have usurped the grounds they now possess, and from which they have dislodged several nations in order to make way for their building of cities, villages, and forts. . . .

Be it known to you, Onnonthio, that for the future you ought to take care, that with so great a number of martial men as I now see, being shut up in so small a fort, do not stifle and choke the Tree of Peace. Since it took root so easily, it must needs be of pernicious consequence to stop its growth, and hinder it from shading both your country and ours with its leaves. I do assure you, in the name of the Five Nations, that our warriors shall dance the Calumet Dance* under its branches; that they shall rest in tranquility upon their mats, and will never dig up the axe to cut down the Tree of Peace, until such time as the Onnonthio and the Corlaer do either jointly or separately offer to invade the country that the Great Spirit has given to our ancestors.

---

*A dance in celebration of the calumet, or peace pipe, which established a ritual kinship between the performer/s and the person/s in whose honor the dance was given.

65

A Swedish visualization of the 17th-century Eastern Indians. From Holm, Kort Beskrifning. Rare Books and Manuscripts Division, NYPL.

1689

When the Abenaki Indians living east of the Hudson River (referred to as the "Eastern Indians" by the English) allied themselves with the French, agents for the Massachusetts Bay, New-Plymouth, and Connecticut colonies went to Albany in an attempt to secure the cooperation of the Five Nations. On 24 September, Tahajadoris, a Mohawk sachem, pledged continuing friendship to the English, and swore unceasing hostility against the French, but declined to join in an action against the Abenakis.

> Brethren,
> . . . We patiently bore many injuries from the French, from one year to another, before we took up the axe against them. Our patience made the governor of Canada think that we were afraid of him, and dared not resent the injuries we had so long suffered; but now he is undeceived. We assure you that we are resolved never to drop the axe; the French shall never see our faces in peace, we shall never be reconciled as long as one Frenchman is alive. We shall never make peace, though our nation should be ruined by it, and every one of us cut in pieces. Our brethren of the three colonies may depend on this. . . .
> As to what you told us of the Owenagungas [Abenakis] and Uragees [Mahicans], we answer that we were never so proud and haughty, as to begin a war without just provocation. You tell us that they are treacherous rogues—we believe it—and that they will undoubtedly assist the French. If they shall do this, or shall join with any of our enemies, either French or Indians, then we shall kill and destroy them. . . .

Adario and Baron de Lahontan compare European and Indian attitudes to life. From Louis-Armand de Lahontan, Dialogues . . . *(Amsterdam, 1704), frontispiece. Rare Books and Manuscripts Division, NYPL.*

1690

Adario (called Kondarionk by his own people, and "The Rat" by the French) was an outstanding Huron chief who often acted as peacemaker and diplomat for the French during Frontenac's War (1689–97). Having lived in France, as well as in New York and Quebec, Adario felt that he was qualified to discuss the customs of both the English and the French. He spent considerable time with Baron Louis-Armand de Lahontan, a French explorer who became lieutenant governor of Placentia, in Newfoundland. After the Frenchman had criticized Adario for preferring the Huron way of life, saying that Hurons "have no more than the shape of men," and that severe laws were needed to punish the wicked, while honesty produced its own reward, Adario replied:

> Ay, ay, my dear brother, your being an honest man would not avail you if two false witnesses swear against you, you'll presently see whether your laws are severe or not. Have not the *coureurs de bois* quoted me twenty instances of persons that have been cruelly

put to death by the lash of your laws, whose innocence has appeared after their death? What truth is there in their relations, I do not pretend to know; but it is plain that such a thing may happen. I have heard them say further (and indeed I had heard the same thing in France before) that poor innocent men are tortured in a most horrible manner, in order to force them by the violence of their torment to a confession of all that is charged upon them and of ten times more. What execrable tyranny this must be! Though the French pretend to be men, yet the women are not exempted from this horrid cruelty, any more than the men; both the one and the other choose rather to die once than to die fifty times. And indeed they are in the right of it. For if it should happen that by the influence of extraordinary courage, they were capable of undergoing such torments without confessing a crime that they never committed, what health, what manner of life can they enjoy thereafter? No, no, my dear brother, the black devils that the Jesuits talk so much of are not in the regions where souls burn in flames, but in Quebec and in France, where they keep company with the laws, the false witnesses, the conveniences of life, the cities, the fortresses, and the pleasures you spoke of but now.

1692

When they renewed their covenant with the English in 1692, the Iroquois asked for guns so that they could protect themselves from the Hurons, who were well supplied with both guns and powder by the French. Offering them only ammunition, the English said that the Indians had been careless with the guns they had previously received. The Iroquois replied sharply to Major Richard Ingoldsby, the interim English governor of New York, when they conferred with him in June.

Let us not reproach one another, such words do not savor well among friends. . . .

We return you thanks for the powder and lead given us; but what shall we do without guns, shall we throw them at the enemy? We doubt they will not hurt them so. Before this we always had guns given us. It is no wonder the governor of Canada gains upon us, for he supplies his Indians with guns as well as powder; he supplies them plentifully with everything that can hurt us.

Guerrier Iroquois

A fully armed Iroquois warrior, carrying both a war hatchet and a rifle. An engraving by Laroque, from an illustration by J. Grasset St. Sauveur. Courtesy of The New-York Historical Society, New York City.

3

The 18th Century
"They want to make husbandmen of our warriors."

Eighteenth-century Europe was a continent filled with contrasts and contradictions. The spirit of the Enlightenment had spread widely—England and
France enjoyed close cultural ties, and Empress Maria Theresa of Austria
strove to improve the lot of the serfs in her dominions. Yet much of the
century was scarred by a succession of politically motivated, inconclusive,
and destructive wars.

The structure of power in the New World was changing. By the terms of
the Peace of Utrecht (1713), the French ceded Acadia, Newfoundland, and
the Hudson Bay Territory to England, along with the tribes constituting the
Five Nations. Without their consent, these Indians were declared British
subjects. The Spanish were rapidly losing lands they had conquered during
the 15th and 16th centuries. When the Jesuits were ordered out of New
Spain in 1767, the mission villages which they had founded fell to ruin, and
their social programs disintegrated as well. With the expulsion of the Jesuits,
Spain lost its greatest influence over the Indians and its most cohesive force
in Spanish America. The French, however, continued to trade profitably in
fur, and generally remained on good terms with the Indians. And with their
purchase of Manhattan Island for $24.00 in trade goods in 1624, the Dutch
had initiated the practice of buying land from the Indians, a method later
adopted by the English in Rhode Island and by the Quakers in Pennsylvania.

In addition to claiming sovereignty over the Indians by fiat, as above, the
English also fostered intertribal warfare, for, divided against each other, the
Indians were less able to protect their lands against the English. A treaty
with England often meant the beginning of English incursions on lands that
were still nominally Indian property. These practices led to hostility and
reprisals on both sides, and finally to indiscriminate bloodshed.

Increasingly provoked by the white men's insatiable land hunger and the
extent to which they would go to defraud the Indians of their heritage,
Indians like the Delaware Teedyuscung (or Kekeuscung, "The Healer," or
"Earth Trembler") spoke up in council meetings held with white officials,
openly confronting the latter with the blatant inconsistencies of their race.

Such Indian leaders reiterated in vain the many ways in which Indian friendship, hospitality, and assistance had been repaid with deceit and persecution. Still, those Indians taken to Europe early in the century acted as diplomatic envoys, preparing for renewed attempts to negotiate peace treaties through which, when they were negotiated, the Indians were destined to lose ever more of their lands and possessions.

European powers battled fiercely for control of the profitable Indian trade, as well as the Indian land. In the process, a Dutch governor is said to have initiated what later became a popular practice—offering bounties for Indian scalps. In 1725, a group of New Hampshire militiamen scalped a party of sleeping Indians, and were later rewarded for their "heroism" by the city of Dover with the sum of £100 for each scalp. Even Pennsylvania, with its reputation for tolerance, was offering bounties for Indian scalps as late as 1764.

Although in the early years of the century many Indians were still refusing to learn any of the white men's ways, some felt that participation in the European educational system could provide a valuable tool to aid the survival of their people by allowing them to be more articulate, better-equipped spokesmen for their people in their dealings with the Europeans. New Indian leaders arose in the English colonies. Outstanding among them was the Shawnee chief Tecumseh (or Tecumtha, "Crouching Tiger"), who would become an even more prominent figure in the 19th century. Fluent in English and widely read in English history and literature, he constantly promoted the cause of peace, but found death in the Battle of the Thames in 1813.

The English, French, and Dutch continued to defraud the Indians throughout the century. "Friendship" and "treaties" as well as outright purchases continued to cut away at the Indians' landholdings. After the infamous "Walking Purchase," in which the Indians granted the English as much land as a white man could walk in a day, only to find that the Europeans were using specially trained, professional "walkers," the Indians realized that a tribal alliance would strengthen their bargaining power in dealing with governors, traders, and missionaries and increase their abilities to resist the attacks of European military contingents.

British-French rivalry climaxed in 1753, with the outbreak of the French and Indian War (the most decisive in a series of wars beginning in 1689), in which all Indian tribes except the Iroquois sided with the French. In an attempt to win the Indians over to their side, the British instituted a new policy, aimed at providing fair treatment for the Indians. However, the Indians' earlier fears of the British were heightened by the French-spread rumors that the English were planning to exterminate them. Desperately, the Indians attempted to surmount tribal differences. At last they took up arms to prevent the further encroachment of the English and other whites inland from the eastern seacoast, and to prevent the total distintegration of Indian tribal life.

This situation inspired Pontiac, the charismatic Ottawa leader and orator, to try to coordinate all Indian tribes in one massive final campaign against the white men. With the support of the Algonquins, Senecas, Mingos, and Wyandots, he led an uprising in 1763, capturing nine of the twelve British forts west of Fort Niagara, in New York, and also laying siege to Detroit for six months. Unable to recapture the fort, he retreated. This was the decisive defeat in a conflict which continued sporadically for a further two years until Pontiac negotiated a settlement with Sir William Johnson in 1766. In the meantime, the French and Indian War, which gave rise to the rebellion, had ended in a victory for the British. The Proclamation of 1763 set a line of demarcation between Indian and white lands from that time forward, and the British acquired Canada and the vast eastern Louisiana territory. Once again, under this treaty, the Indians were guaranteed their land, rights, and liberty, but there were no enforceable laws to protect them.

By the end of the 18th century, Indian power and cohesion had greatly eroded. Indians were rapidly losing their land to rapacious white settlers, and their numbers were fast diminishing as a result of their increased use of alcohol, and through war and disease. (New diseases to which the Indians had no immunity were brought over by the colonists, and spread rapidly with disastrous results.) Slaves infected with smallpox arrived in Charlestown, South Carolina in 1738. The disease spread to Georgia and by 1750 almost half of the Cherokee tribe had been destroyed by the severe epidemic. Later, during Pontiac's Rebellion, there were persistent rumors that General Jeffrey Amherst, the British commander, who was known to detest the Indians, deliberately planned to spread smallpox among them by giving them contaminated blankets.

Indian exposure to, and assimilation of, white influences was increasing. Some Indians felt that the traditional Indian tribal education was no longer an adequate preparation for their changing world, and that learning more about the white man's ways would help them deal more effectively with the whites. The Indians wanted teachers, and, at their request, the first permanent Indian school was created at Williamsburg, Virginia, in 1720. Three years later so many Indian students were attending the neighboring College of William and Mary that a special building had to be erected to accommodate them. The Indian Charity School, established in 1750 specifically for the education of Indian children, evolved into Dartmouth College, a transformation assisted by a $500 grant from the Continental Congress in 1775.

There was also increasing intermarriage between Indians and whites, and many of the children from these marriages were baptized with Christian first names. Some also assumed the surnames of their white mothers or fathers, and still others adopted names given to them by the whites. Among these were the Indians, like Samson Occum, who studied and traveled abroad, and preached Christianity among their own tribesmen. Well educated, Alexander McGillivray (Hippo-ilk-mico, "The Good Child King"), son of a Scottish father and an Indian mother, became an officer first in the Spanish army and then in the United States army. A man of great wealth, he lived lavishly and called himself "the emperor of the Creeks," the tribe of which he was the ruling chief until his death in 1793.

The whites' strategy of divisive warfare—of pitting one Indian tribe against another to prevent their joining forces—which was to become so characteristic of the next century, was already a part of the Indian war pattern, with Indians joining opposing white forces and ultimately fighting against their own former allies and even against their own tribesmen. By the end of the century, even the powerful Iroquois Confederacy had destroyed itself, through factionalism and allegiance to conflicting groups of whites.

As life in the colonies expanded, it took new directions, diverging from its British origins in interests, ideals, and habits. Each area developed a pattern and rhythm of its own, and each felt steadily more alienated from England.

Among many developing grievances, the most deeply felt was in response to the fact that the agents of the British crown could control the colonies without ever setting foot on American soil. The governor of a royal colony was the agent of the Crown and was required to do what was best for the home government, rather than for the colony. And British colonial officers could have their duties performed by a deputy in the colonies, while they collected their income in England.

It was this lack of sympathy between the colonies and Britain, and of cohesive, beneficial policies, that led to a growing feeling in America that separation was inevitable and that political unity could be achieved only if colonial autonomy were recognized.

In many ways, the colonists' quarrel with Britain was similar to the Indians' quarrel with the whites. In the one case estrangement led to the American Revolution and to the creation of a new nation. But the fledgling American government, too, formulated policies to control Indian-white relations under which the Indians were given short shrift. Made "colonists" in their own country, they continued to lose their lands and autonomy.

There were intermittent attempts at conciliation on the part of the government. In 1778 the Delawares, who had lived for twenty years on the Brotherton Reservation, were offered statehood—a peace treaty with them in Pittsburgh guaranteed them territorial rights, and promised that, under certain conditions, they would be permitted to have a representative in Congress. But on the whole there were more attempts to simply control the Indians. In 1786, the first federal Indian reservation was created, once again under the specious premise that this new restriction of liberty was a way of assuring that the Indians would not suffer any further unlawful seizure of their lands.

But Indian-white wars continued. In 1791 came the worst defeat that white men had ever suffered at the hands of fighting Indians. In a battle that took place on the banks of the Wabash River, Little Turtle (Michikinikwa), at the head of a powerful force of Miamis, was able to rout the 1,400-man U.S. militia led by General Arthur St. Clair. St. Clair's mismanagement of the battle, which resulted in 900 casualties (630 were killed), led to congressional inquiries. In spite of his eventual exoneration from charges of negligence, St. Clair resigned his commission.

Four years later, Little Turtle himself was defeated in Ohio by St. Clair's successor, General "Mad Anthony" Wayne, at the battle of Fallen Timbers. Convinced that they could no longer fight the new American government, Little Turtle and other chiefs met at Fort Greenville, Ohio, with the American peace commissioners and Indian chiefs and warriors. The Treaty of Greenville, signed that day by Little Turtle and the other chiefs, relinquished all Indian claims to a large territory that now comprises a part of Indiana and the entire state of Ohio. The region was opened up to trade and the Indians were offered money and annuities, as well as the opportunity to become "civilized" in the white man's way. The struggle for the preservation of Indian culture and for peace between Indians and whites in contested lands moved farther west, beyond the Mississippi and north to Canada.

At the end of the century, with the traditional Indian way of life rapidly disintegrating, there came hope of its renewal in the form of the cult of Handsome Lake (Ganiodaio), a Seneca prophet. After experiencing a series of visions in which he spoke with supernatural beings, he began to preach the tenets of a new religion. This religion became known as the Code of Handsome Lake (or Kaiwiyoh). It was a syncretic faith combining Quaker religious tenets and traditional Iroquois ways. Certain traditional observances should be retained, it instructed, but evil practices such as drunkenness and witchcraft should be abjured. The Indians should learn about the white men's ways in order to be able to cope more effectively with change; but they should not forget the significant aspects of their own traditional culture. Though at first considered revolutionary, the Code of Handsome Lake was quickly accepted, not only by the Senecas, but by the Onondagas and the Cayugas in New York as well as by Iroquois in Canada. It became a unifying force that helped many Indians resist white importunities that they sell all their lands and move farther and farther west.

The four chiefs who were presented to Queen Anne in 1710: (a) Tee Yee Neen Ho Ga Row. He holds a wampum belt with crosses—a petition for missionaries—and was spokesman for the group. (b) Etow Oh Koam. (c) Ho Nee Yeath Taw No. (d) Sa Ga Yeath Qua Pieth Tow. Mezzotints from portraits by John Verelst (1710). Smithsonian Institution, National Anthropological Archives.

1710

Peter Schuyler, the mayor of Albany, New York, took five Indian chiefs to London. One died en route. The remaining four were King Hendrick (Tee Yee Neen Ho Ga Row, or Thoyanoguen, "He Who Holds the Door Open"), emperor of the Six Nations; Etow Oh Koam, king of the River Nation (as the Mohegans were known); Ho Nee Yeath Taw No, king of the Generethgariches, and Brant (Sa Ga Yeath Pieth Tow), king of the Maquas, or Mohawks, and the grandfather of Joseph Brant (Thayendenagea) who became famous later in the century. They were presented to Queen Anne at a formal ceremony at St. James's Palace, and through an interpreter the Four Kings,* as they came to be known, expressed their distrust of the French, against whom they were preparing to war, and reminded the queen of an earlier promise to send them military assistance:

Great Queen!

We have undertaken a long and tedious voyage, which none of our predecessors could ever be prevailed upon to undertake. The motive that induced us, was that we might see our great Queen, and relate to her those things we thought absolutely necessary, for the good of her, and us, her allies on the other side of the great water. . . .

We were mightily rejoiced when we heard by Anagarjaux, that our great Queen had resolved to send an army to reduce Canada; from whose mouth we readily embraced our great Queen's instructions, and in token of our friendship, we hung up the kettle, and took up the hatchet, and with one consent, joined our brother Queder, Colonel Schuyler, and Anagarjaux, Colonel Nicholson, in making preparations on this side [of] the lake, by building forts, storehouses, canoes, and boats; while Anadiasia, Colonel Vetch, at the same time raised an army at Boston, of which we were informed by our ambassadors, whom we sent thither for that purpose. We waited long in expectation of the fleet from England, to join Anadiasia, Colonel Vetch, then to go against Quebec by sea, while Anagarjaux, Queder, and we went to Port Royal by land; but at last we were told that our great Queen, by some important affair, was prevented in her design for that season.

This made us extremely sorrowful, lest the French, who hitherto had dreaded us, should now think us unable to make war against them. The reduction of Canada is of such weight, that after the effecting thereof, we should have free hunting, and a great trade with our great Queen's children, and as a token of the sincerity of the Six Nations, we do here, in the name of all, present our great Queen with the belts of wampum.

We need not urge to our great Queen, more than the necessity we really labor under obliges us, that in case our great Queen should not be mindful of us, we must with our families forsake our country, and seek other habitations, or stand neutral; either of which will be much against our inclinations.

Since we have been in alliance with our great Queen's children, we have had some knowledge of the Savior of the world, and have often been importuned by the French, both by the insinuations of their priests, and by presents, to come over to their interest, but have always esteemed them men of falsehood. But if our great Queen will be pleased to send over some persons to instruct us, they shall find a most hearty welcome.

We now close, with hopes of our great Queen's favor, and leave it to her most gracious consideration.

*Indian chiefs presented to English kings or queens were always termed "kings" as a mark of respect.

When The Stung Serpent died, Le Page du Pratz drew this sketch of the funeral procession and the ritual strangling of the men who would accompany the Indian in the afterlife. Although the French were horrified by this custom, they were unable to convince the Natchez to discontinue it. Smithsonian Institution, National Anthropological Archives.

1718–23

Le Page du Pratz, a French traveler, spent five years among the Natchez, who then lived in the southern part of the present state of Mississippi. He became a close friend of The Stung Serpent, a high-ranking noble, who bitterly complained that the Indians had been much better off before the French came.

Why did the French come into our country? We did not go to seek them. They asked land of us, because their country was too little for all the men that were in it. We told them they might take land where they pleased, there was enough for them and for us; that it was good the same sun should enlighten us both, and that we should walk as friends, in the same path, and that we would give them of our provisions, assist them to build, and to labor in their fields. We have done so; is not this true? What occasion, then, had we for Frenchmen? Before they came, did we not live better than we do, seeing we deprive ourselves of a part of our corn, our game, and fish, to give a part to them? In what respect, then, had we occasion for them? Was it for their guns? The bows and arrows, which we used, were sufficient to make us live well. Was it for their white, blue, and red blankets? We can do well enough with buffalo skins which are warmer; our women wrought feather blankets for the winter, and mulberry mantles for the summer; which indeed were not so beautiful, but our women were more laborious and less vain than they are now. In fine, before the arrival of the French we lived like men who can be satisfied with what they have; whereas at this day we are like slaves, who are not suffered to do as they please.

1730

In an effort to gain the support of the Cherokees against the French, Sir Alexander Cuming had Chief Moytoy of the Cherokee village of Tellico, in Tennessee, crowned "emperor of the Cherokee," giving him control over the seven principal Cherokee towns. In June, a month after Moytoy's coronation, Cuming took seven Cherokee chiefs to London, where they were formally presented to George II. On 7 September they signed a treaty of peace in the name of the entire Cherokee Nation. One of the chiefs, Ketagustah, speaking on behalf of the whole group, later explained to Cuming their reasons for agreeing to remain friendly with the English:

> We are come thither from a mountainous place, where nothing but darkness is to be found, but we are now in a place where there is light. There was a person in our country, he gave us a yellow token of warlike honor [a gold medal], which is left with Moytoy of Telliquo, and as warriors we received it. He came to us like a warrior from you. A man he is; his talk is upright, and the token he left preserves his memory among us. We look upon you as if the great king were present; we love you as representing the great king. We shall die in the same way of thinking. The crown of our nation is different from that which the great King George wears, and from what we saw in the tower. But to us it is all one. The chain of friendship shall be carried to our people. We look upon the great King George as the sun, and as our father, and upon ourselves as his children. For though we are red, and you are white, yet our hands and hearts are joined together. When we shall have acquainted our people with what we have seen, our children from generation to generation will always remember it. In war we shall always be one with you. The enemies of the great king shall be our enemies. His people and ours shall be one, and shall die together. We came hither naked and poor as the worms of the earth, but you have everything, and we that have nothing must love you, and will never break the chain of friendship which is between us. . . . This small rope [wampum] we show you is all that we have to bind our slaves with, and it may be broken. But you have iron chains for yours. However, if we catch your slaves, we will bind them as well as we can, and deliver them to our friends, and take no pay for it. We have looked round for the person that was in our country—he is not here. However, we must say he talked uprightly to us, and we shall never forget him. Your white people may safely build houses near us. We shall hurt nothing that belongs to them, for we are children of one father, the great king, and shall live and die together.

Cherokee Indians brought to London by Sir Alexander Cuming. Left to right: O. Onaconoa, K. Skalilosken Ketagustah, K. Kollana, O. K. Oukah Ulah, T. Tathtowe, C. Clogoittah, U. Ukwaneequa. An engraving by Isaac Basire, from a painting by Markham. Smithsonian Institution, National Anthropological Archives.

Tomochichi and his nephew Tooanahowi in London. A mezzotint by John Faber from a portrait by Willem Verelst (1734). Smithsonian Institution, National Anthropological Archives.

1734

General James Oglethorpe took a deputation of thirteen Creeks to England, hoping to reinforce friendly relations in his colony of Georgia. Among the deputation were Tomochichi, the *mico*, or principal chief, Senawki, his wife, and Tooanahowi, his nephew. Special suits of clothing were made for the Indians, and they were presented to George II by Sir Clement Cotterel, the king's master of ceremonies. After offering the king the ceremonial eagle's feathers, Tomochichi expressed the wish of the entire Creek Nation for a lasting peace:

> This day I see the majesty of your face, the greatness of your house, and the number of your people. I am come for the good of the whole nation of the Creeks, to renew the peace they had long ago made with the English. I am come over in my old days, and, though I cannot live to see any advantage to myself, I am come for the good of the children of all the nations of the Upper and Lower Creeks, that they may be instructed in the knowledge of the English. These are the feathers of the eagle, which is the swiftest of birds, and flies all around our nations. These feathers are a sign of peace in our land, and we have brought them over to leave them with you, great king, as a sign of everlasting peace. Oh! great king, whatsoever words you shall say unto me, I will tell them faithfully to all the kings of the Creek nations.

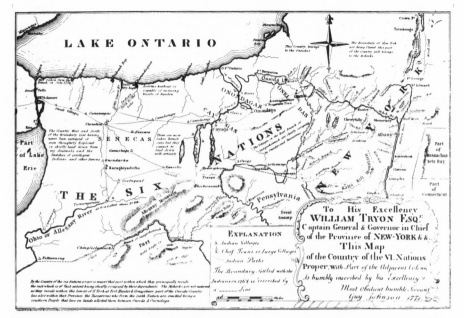

18th-century map by Guy Johnson showing the extent of the land controlled by the Six Nations after the treaty described below and a series of similar ones concluding in the year 1768. From Edmund B. Callaghan, Documentary History of the State of New York (Albany, N.Y., 1851). Courtesy of The New-York Historical Society, New York City.

1742

Canassatego, a Seneca chief, was outspoken in his denunciation of the lies and cheating of the white men. On 7 July, he addressed a large council meeting of Indians and whites in Philadelphia, speaking on behalf of the Six Nations (as the Iroquois Confederacy was called after 1715, when the original Five Nations was officially joined by the Tuscaroras). He berated the whites for the inadequate compensation his people had received from them for lands ceded to them, particularly in Maryland and Virginia, and for other abuses to which all whites, with the exception of William Penn, with whom they had negotiated their original treaty, and regarded as the ultimate authority, had subjected the confederacy.

> Brethren, . . . You yesterday put us in mind, first, of William Penn's early and constant care to cultivate friendship with all the Indians; of the treaty we held with one of his sons, about ten years ago, and of the necessity there is at this time of keeping the roads between us clear and free from all obstructions. . . .
>
> You, in the next place, said you would enlarge the fire [of friendship] and make it burn brighter. . . .
>
> In the last place, you were pleased to say that we are bound by the strictest leagues to watch for each other's preservation. . . . This is equally agreeable to us; and we shall not fail to give you

81

early intelligence, whenever anything of consequence comes to our knowledge. . . .

Brethren, we received from the proprietors [Penn and his sons] yesterday some goods in consideration of our release of the lands on the west side of [the] Susquehanna. It is true, we have the full quantity according to agreement; but if the proprietor had been here himself, we think, in regard to our numbers and poverty, he would have made an addition to them. If the goods were only to be divided among the Indians present, a single person would have but a small portion; but if you consider what numbers are left behind, equally entitled with us to a share, there will be extremely little. We therefore desire, if you have the keys of the proprietor's chest, you will open it and take out a little more for us.

We know our lands are now become more valuable. The white people think we do not know their value; but we are sensible that the land is everlasting, and the few goods we receive for it are soon worn out and gone. For the future, we will sell no lands but when Brother Onas [William Penn] is in the country; and we will know beforehand the quantity of the goods we are to receive. Besides, we are not well used with respect to the lands still unsold by us. Your people daily settle on these lands, and spoil our hunting. We must insist on your removing them, as you know they have no right to settle to the northward of the Kittochtinny Hills. . . .*

We have further to observe, . . . that though Brother Onas (meaning the Proprietor) has paid us for what his people possess, yet some parts of that country have been taken up by persons whose place of residence is to the south of this province, from whom we have never received any consideration. . . .

As we have never heard from you on this head [matter], we want to know what you have done on it. If you have not done anything, we renew our request, and desire you will inform the person whose people are seated on our lands that that country belongs to us, in right of conquest, we having bought it with our blood, and taken it from our enemies in fair war, and we expect, as owners of that land, to receive such a consideration for it as the land is worth. . . . Let him say "Yes" or "No;" if he says "Yes," we will treat with him; if "No," we are able to do ourselves justice, and we will do it by going to take payment.

---

*The Kittatiny Mountains, a 2,000-foot ridge in New Jersey and Pennsylvania, had been set as the boundary line between the English settlements and Indian land.

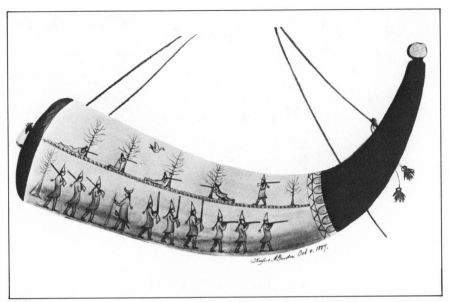

Detail from an 18-century powder horn, such as was used by the English fighting Tanacharison, showing European and Indian methods of warfare. Courtesy of The New-York Historical Society, New York City.

1753

Tanacharison (called "The Half King" because he acted as a deputy for the Iroquois in lands the Iroquois had conquered), was an Oneida chief who played an important role in the French war against the English in western Pennsylvania. When the increasing power of the British gradually forced the French to strengthen many of their outpost garrisons, the forces of Tanacharison and his followers were correspondingly weakened.

At Fort Le Boeuf on French Creek (now Waterford, Pennsylvania), Tanacharison warned Commander Pierre Paul, Sieur de Marin, that the French were now intruding upon Indian lands, contrary to the agreement they had made with the Indians in Montreal in 1688.

> Fathers, we kindled a fire a long time ago, at a place called Montreal, where we desired you to stay, and not to come and intrude upon our land.
>
> I now desire you may dispatch to that place, for be it known to you, Fathers, that this land is our land, not yours. . . .
>
> I tell you in plain words you must go off this land. You say you have a strong body, a strong neck, and a strong voice, that when you speak all the Indians must hear you. It is true you are a strong body and ours is but weak, yet we are not afraid of you. We forbid you to come any further; turn back to the place from whence you came.

83

Johnson Hall, in Johnstown, New York, with Indians gathered on the lawn. *Photograph, owned by John B. Knox, of a painting by E. L. Henry (1903). Collection Albany Institute of History and Art.*

1753

Sir William Johnson, British superintendent of Indian affairs in the northern colonies, was dearly beloved of the Indians. He took a personal interest in Indian affairs, and participated actively in the British expeditions against the French in Canada. An honorary sachem of the Mohawks, and a major general in the British provincial forces, he had rallied the Six Nations in both King George's War (1744–48) and the French and Indian War.

At his family mansion, Johnson Hall (Johnstown, New York), Johnson frequently welcomed both Europeans and Indians. Indians held council meetings on the lawn, where they felt free to discuss their problems with him, as they did when they met him in council elsewhere.

Alarmed by the constant inroads being made on Indian lands, the great Mohawk chief King Hendrick (Thoyanoguen) protested to the authorities in Albany about the wrongs that had been done to the Indians, only to have his requests for fair treatment ignored. Angrily, he declared that Indian ties to the English were severed. At this point, the English in Albany, aware that the situation had been precipitated by their own inept handling of the tribes, asked Johnson for his help.

Johnson traveled to Onondaga, the Indians' principal meeting ground, to attempt to pacify Hendrick. He found the chiefs angry and confused, and Hendrick spoke for all of them when, at a meeting on 10 September, he exclaimed:

> We don't know what you Christians, English and French, intend. We are so hemmed in by you both that we have hardly a hunting place left. In a little while, if we find a bear in a tree, there will immediately appear an owner of the land to claim the property and hinder us from killing it, by which we live. We are so perplexed between you that we hardly know what to say or think.

A Mohawk Indian. Courtesy of the American Museum of Natural History.

1754

For almost ten years, the Mohawks had been complaining about the duplicity of the Indian commissioners at Albany, and many Anglo-Indian conferences had been held there in an effort to arrive at an understanding. In June and July, a major meeting was held in Albany, at which New York's Lieutenant Governor James De Lancey presided as official host.

On 27 June, Canadagaia, a Mohawk chief, addressed De Lancey, complaining about the illegal seizure of the tribes' lands and demanding that the Indians be given the same fair treatment that had been offered by them to the colonists:

Brother . . .

We shall now open our minds, and we beg you will take time to consider what we shall say and not give us too hasty an answer or in two or three words, and then turn your back upon us. As you are a new governor, we beg you will treat us tenderly and not as the former governor did, who turned his back upon us before we knew he intended to depart, so that we had no opportunity to finish our business with him. The reason we desire you would treat us in this tender manner, is because this is the place where we are to expect a redress of our grievances and we hope all things will be so settled that we may part good friends.

Brother,

We told you a little while ago that we had an uneasiness on our minds and we shall now tell you what it is. It is concerning our land. We understand that there were writings [treaties] for all our lands so that we shall have none left but the very spot we live upon, and hardly that. We have examined among the elderly people who are now present if they have sold any of it, who deny that they have. And we earnestly desire you will take this into consideration, which will give us great satisfaction, and convince us that you have a friendship for us. We don't complain of those who have honestly bought the land they possess, or those to whom we have given any, but to some who have taken more than we have given them. We find we are very poor; we thought we had yet land round about us, but it is said there are writings for it all. It is one condition of the ancient covenant chain, that if there be any uneasiness on either side or any request to be made, that they shall be considered with a brotherly regard. And we hope you will fulfill this condition on your side, as we shall always be ready to do on ours. We have embraced this opportunity of unbosoming ourselves to you with regard to our castle [fortified village] and we are well assured that the other castle of the Mohawks have complaints of the same nature to make when they come down. We have now declared our own grievances and the Casajoharys will declare theirs, but that we shall leave to them. By this belt [wampum] we desire you to consider what we have said; and by the same we inform you that the Five Nations* have something to say to you before you speak to them. . . .

*The Tuscaroras were not involved in this conflict.

86

King Hendrick. An engraving from an original drawing by T. Jeffreys (1756). Courtesy of The New-York Historical Society.

1754

At the Albany council meeting, King Hendrick also spoke for his tribe. Though he now reaffirmed his relationship with the English, he was by this time wary of their protestations of brotherhood. In his speech, he presented a list of legitimate Indian grievances, stating—as Canadagaia had—that the whites had defrauded the Mohawks of their lands; had supplied them with too much rum, but too few useful gifts; that the people of Pennsylvania and

Virginia were encroaching on Iroquois lands in the western part of those colonies; and that Albany traders were selling arms to the French and at the same time urging the Iroquois nation to attack them. But his speech was also a heartfelt plea for faith and support from the whites with whom he at one time had shared such a strong bond of friendship. It was printed in the *Gentlemen's Magazine* and in the provincial newspapers, and it made him famous.

> We do now solemnly renew and brighten the covenant chain.*
> We shall take the chain belt to Onondaga [New York], where our council fire always burns, and keep it so safe that neither thunder nor lightning shall break it.
>
> It is true that we live disunited. We have tried to bring back our brethren, but in vain, for the governor of Canada is like a wicked, deluding spirit. You ask why we are so dispersed. The reason is that you have neglected us for these three years past. [At this point he took out a stick and threw it behind him.] You have thus thrown us behind your back; whereas the French are a subtle and vigilant people, always using their utmost endeavors to seduce and bring us over to them. . . .
>
> The governor of Virginia and the governor of Canada are quarreling about lands which belong to us, and their quarrel may end in our destruction. . . . Look about your country and see: You have no fortifications, no, not even in this city. It is but a step from Canada here, and the French may come and turn you out of doors. You desire us to speak from the bottom of our hearts and we shall do it. But you are all like women, bare and open, without fortifications.

---

*The Indian-white confederation, known as the Covenant Chain. The agreement was reinforced by the gift of a belt, or chain, of wampum.

1756

On 13 November, at a meeting held in Albany, Teedyuscung, a famous Delaware chief, was asked by Colonel William Denny, the newly arrived British governor of Pennsylvania, and the Quaker commissioners, who signed treaties on behalf of the Quaker community, whether any of the previous governors or the people of Pennsylvania had ever done the Indians any harm. He replied by accusing the white men of continuously stealing Indian lands. Striking the ground with his foot as he spoke, Teedyuscung declared:

> This very ground that is under me was my [i.e., the Delawares'] land and inheritance, and is taken from me by fraud; when I say this ground, I mean all the land lying between Tohiccon Creek and Wyoming, on the River Susquehanna. I have not only been

Delaware Indians in traditional dress. A sketch by George Catlin. Courtesy of The New-York Historical Society, New York City.

served so in this government, but the same thing has been done to me as to several tracts in New Jersey over the river. When I have sold lands fairly, I look upon them to be really sold—a bargain is a bargain. Though I have sometimes had nothing for the lands I have sold but broken pipes, or such trifles, yet when I have sold them, though for such trifles, I look upon the bargain to be good; yet I think I should not be ill used on this account by those very people who have had such an advantage in their purchases, nor be called a fool for it. . . .

When one man had formerly liberty to purchase lands, and he took the deed from the Indians for it, and then dies, after his death, the children forge a deed, like the true one, with the same Indian names to it, and thereby take lands from the Indians which they never sold—this is fraud. Also, when one king has land beyond the river, and another king has land on this side, both bounded by rivers, mountains, and springs, which cannot be moved, and the proprietaries, greedy to purchase lands, buy of one king what belongs to the other—this likewise is fraud. . . . I have been served so in this province. All the land, extending from Tohiccon over the great mountain [the Appalachian Mountains] to Wyoming has been taken from me by fraud; for when I had agreed to sell the land to the old proprietary by the course of the river, the young proprietaries came and got it run by a straight course by the compass, and by that means took in double the quantity intended to be sold.

Pontiac in council. The Public Archives of Canada.

1763

The Ottawa chief Pontiac was a superb orator as well as warrior. Always an ally of the French, he was incensed at the way in which the English mistreated the Indians. On 5 May, fomenting the rebellion that bears his name, he addressed a group of Potawatomies, Hurons, and Ottawas assembled in a Potawatomie village, which was located on an island in the Detroit River across from Fort Detroit, urging them to take up arms against the English.

It is important for us, my brothers, that we exterminate from our lands this nation which seeks only to destroy us. You see as well as I that we can no longer supply our needs, as we have done from our brothers, the French. The English sell us goods twice as dear as the French do, and their goods do not last. Scarcely have we bought a blanket or something else to cover ourselves with before we must think of getting another; and when we wish to set out for our winter camp they do not want to give us any credit as our brothers the French do.

When I go to see the English commander and say to him that some of our comrades are dead, instead of bewailing their death, as our French brothers do, he laughs at me and at you. If I ask for anything for our sick, he refuses with the reply that he has no use for us. From all this you can well see that they are seeking our ruin. Therefore, my brothers, we must all swear their destruction and wait no longer. Nothing prevents us: They are few in numbers, and we can accomplish it.

All the nations who are our brothers attack them—why should we not strike too? Are we not men like them? Have I not shown you the wampum belts which I received from our great father, the Frenchman [Louis XV]? He tells us to strike them. Why do we not listen to his words? What do we fear? It is time.

Delaware and Mahican Indians being baptized at a Moravian mission in Bethlehem, Pennsylvania. From Kurze, zuverlässige Nachricht von der . . . Kirche Unitas fratrum . . . (1762). Rare Books and Manuscripts Division, NYPL.

1764

When some Wyandots and Delawares moved from Pennsylvania to Ohio, they allowed the Moravians to establish mission stations in their new villages along the banks of the Muskingum River. The following year, the Moravians requested more plots of ground than they had originally asked for. The Indians refused to give it to them. At a council meeting between the Moravians and the Indians, Delaware chief King Beaver (Tamaqué) challenged them, saying:

> Brother! Last year you asked our leave to come and live with us, for the purpose of instructing us and our children, to which we consented, and now being come, we are glad to see you. Brother! It appears to us that you must since have changed your mind; for instead of instructing us or our children, you are cutting down trees on our land; you have marked out a large spot of land for a plantation, as the white people do everywhere . . . and the next thing will be, that a fort will be built. . . . Our country will be claimed by the white people, and we driven further back, as has been the case ever since the white people came.

Indian resentment, sparked by the colonists' refusal to withdraw from traditional hunting grounds west of the Appalachian Mountains, eventually escalated into Lord Dunmore's War. Its chief protagonist was the Mingo chief John Logan (Tah-gah-jute, "His Eyelashes Stick Out or Above" or "Spying") who had in the past been friendly with the whites. But in this year some of Logan's relations, who were with a peaceful hunting party camped at the mouth of the Yellow Creek, in Ohio, were brutally massacred without provocation by a group of whites led by Colonel Michael Cresap, and a few days later the rest of his family was similarly slaughtered. Logan set out to avenge them, attacking white settlements in retaliation. This marked the beginning of the war, which ended in a decisive defeat for the Indians, and resulted in the opening up of the Muskingum River area to further white settlement.

Embittered by the brutal and senseless killing of Indian women and children, and by his own capture, Logan dictated a letter to an interpreter named Gibson, to be taken to Lord Dunmore, the governor of the colony of Virginia. This letter was widely reported in the press, and was later copied by Thomas Jefferson, who had it reprinted in his *Notes on the State of Virginia*. It also appeared in Washington Irving's *The Sketch Book of Geoffrey Crayon, Gent.*, and is an outstanding example of forceful Indian eloquence.

I appeal to any white man to say, if he ever entered Logan's cabin hungry, and he gave him not meat; if ever he came cold and naked, and he clothed him not.

During the course of the last long and bloody war, Logan remained idle in his cabin, an advocate for peace. Such was my love for the whites, that my countrymen pointed as they passed, and said, "Logan is the friend of white men." I had even thought to have lived with you but for the injuries of one man, Colonel Cresap, in cold blood and unprovoked, murdered all the relations of Logan, not even sparing my women and children. There runs not a drop of my blood in the veins of any living creature. This called on me for revenge. I have sought it; I have killed many; I have glutted my vengeance. For my country, I rejoice at the beams of peace. But do not harbor a thought that this is the joy of fear. Logan never felt fear. He will not turn on his heel to save his life. Who is there to mourn for Logan?—Not one!

John Logan. *General Research Division, NYPL.*

A stockaded Six Nations village on the banks of the Susquehanna River. 18th-century villages were very similar. From Arnoldus Montanus, De Nieuwe en Onbekende Weereld (Amsterdam, 1671). Courtesy of The New-York Historical Society, New York City.

1774

The chiefs of the Six Nations protested strongly to Benjamin Franklin about the alienation of their young men, and the imposition of European values by those entrusted with the formal education of Indian youth. One of them observed:

> But you, who are wise, must know that different nations have different conceptions of things; and you will therefore not take it amiss, if our ideas of this kind of education happen not to be the same with yours. We have had some experience of it—several of our young people were formerly brought up at the colleges of the northern provinces; they were instructed in all your sciences, but when they came back to us, they were bad runners, ignorant of every means of living in the woods, unable to bear either cold or hunger, knew neither how to build a cabin, take a deer, or kill an enemy, spoke our language imperfectly, were therefore neither fit for hunters, warriors, nor counsellors; they were totally good for nothing. We are however not the less obliged by your kind offer, though we decline accepting it, and, to show our grateful sense of it, if the gentlemen of Virginia will send us a dozen of their sons, we will take great care of their education, instruct them in all we know, and make *men* of them.

Samson Occum when he was in England raising money for Dartmouth College. A mezzotint by M. Chamberlin from a painting by John Silsbury (1768). Smithsonian Institution, National Portrait Gallery.

1776

Joseph Johnson, a Mohegan educated for missionary work, and Samson Occum ("The Other Side"), the famous Mohegan preacher, had each discussed with various members of the tribe problems that had arisen regarding the lands along the Thames River in Massachusetts that had been taken from them by the English. Knowing that Johnson planned to go to Cambridge to ask George Washington, who was in military camp there, for advice about dealing with the English (Washington had become acquainted with the Indians when he was a surveyor), Occum wrote a letter to Johnson, warning him that George III's ultimate goal was to enslave the Indians, and telling him to try to persuade the tribe not to interfere or participate in the quarrels between the colonists and the English.

> The former kings of England used to let the people of this country have their freedom and liberty, but the present king of England wants to make them slaves to himself, and the people of this country don't want to be slaves, and so they are come over to kill them, and the people here are obliged to defend themselves. Use all your influence with your brethren not to intermeddle in these quarrels among the white people.

95

A *contemporary satirical illustration showing Indians bringing scalps to the English. Detail from an 18th-century powder horn. Courtesy of The New-York Historical Society, New York City.*

1781

In a sarcastic speech that revealed his complete disbelief in the probity of his "allies," Captain Pipe (Hopocam, "Tobacco Pipe"), a Delaware, agreed to support the British against the colonists. At a council meeting held in Detroit in November, he addressed Lieutenant Colonel Henry Hamilton, the British commandant, who was called "The Hair Buyer," because he paid hard cash for scalps—enough in itself to brand him a dubious ally.

> Father, some time ago you put a war hatchet into my hands, saying "Take this weapon and try it on the heads of my enemies, the long knives [American colonists], and let me afterwards know if it was sharp and good." Father, at the time you gave me this weapon, I had neither cause nor inclination to go to war against a people who had done me no injury; yet in obedience to you, who say you are my father, and call me your child, I received the hatchet, well knowing that if I did not obey, you would withhold from me the necessaries of life, without which I could not subsist, and which are not elsewhere to be procured, but at the house of my father. You may perhaps think me a fool, for risking my life at your bidding, in a cause, too, by which I have no prospect of gaining anything; for it is *your* cause and not mine. . . . You should not compel your children, the Indians, to expose themselves for *your* sake.
>
> . . . While you, father, are setting me on your enemy, much in the same manner as a hunter sets his dog on the game . . . I may, perchance, happen to look back to the place from whence you started me, and what shall I see? Perhaps I may see my father shaking hands with the long knives; yes, with these very people he now calls his enemies. I may then see him laugh at my folly for having obeyed his orders; and yet I am now risking my life at his command! . . . I have done with the hatchet what you ordered me to do, and found it sharp. Nevertheless, I did not do *all* that I *might* have done. . . . I felt compassion for *your* enemy. . . . I spared [him].

Fort Harmar, near present-day Marietta, Ohio, built in 1785, was the site of many council meetings between the Delawares and the whites. With the Reverend Heckewelder acting as interpreter, the two groups met in the small council house depicted at the extreme left of this picture. Detail from an 18th-century powder horn. Courtesy of The New-York Historical Society, New York City.

1781

When the Delaware chief Pachgantsilias (or Buckongehelas, "Breaker in Pieces") spoke in council to the Indians at Gnadenhutten (now Pennsylvania) in April, he reviewed the history of the relations between the whites and the Delawares. Telling the tribe to leave their homes, which he said were exposed to constant danger from attack by the whites, he pleaded with them to seek safety among the Wyandots, who lived on the Maumee River in Ohio. The Delawares refused to leave and said they had nothing to fear, since they had always had amicable relations with the whites in Pennsylvania. The Reverend John Heckewelder, a Moravian missionary and interpreter who had lived with the Pennsylvania Indians for many years, recorded Pachgantsilias's speech, which proved to be prophetic, for eleven months later the entire Indian community of Gnadenhutten was brutally massacred by a band of white marauders.

> I admit there are good white men, but they bear no proportion to the bad; the bad must be the strongest, for they rule. They do what they please. They enslave those who are not of their color, although created by the same Great Spirit who created us. They would make slaves of us if they could, but as they cannot do it, they kill us! There is no faith to be placed in their words. They are not like the Indians, who are only enemies, while at war, and are friends in peace. They will say to an Indian, "my friend! my brother!" They will take him by the hand, and at the same moment destroy him. And so you [addressing himself to the Christian Indians] will also be treated by them before long. Remember that this day I have warned you to beware of such friends as these. I know the long knives [the white men]; they are not to be trusted.

In 1784, commissioners representing New York, Pennsylvania, and the Congress of the newly established United States had induced the Six Nations with whom they had been fighting to sign the Treaty of Fort Stanwix (at Rome, New York). In spite of the objections of chief Red Jacket, who openly distrusted the intentions of the commissioners, and thinking that peace at any price was preferable to continued warfare, Seneca chief Cornplanter (Kaiiwontwakon, "By What One Plants") signed the treaty, by whose terms the Senecas lost large portions of their lands in New York and Pennsylvania. In return for his cooperation, Cornplanter was rewarded with a yearly stipend and the grant of a reservation in Pennsylvania bearing his name.

But the Senecas were really dissatisfied with the terms of the treaty, and in this year the chiefs Big Tree, Half-Town, and Cornplanter sent a message to George Washington to complain about them and to justify their earlier support of the English during the Revolutionary War. They also chastised Washington for ordering General John Sullivan's punitive expedition into Six Nations territory during the war with instructions to totally destroy the Indian settlements and take all the survivors as hostages. This act had earned him the name Canotaucarius, "The Town Destroyer," as the chiefs reminded him in this eloquent summary of the events of the past.

Father. The voice of the Seneca nations speaks to you, the great counsellor, in whose heart the wise men of all the thirteen fires [thirteen original states] have placed their wisdom. It may be very small in your ears, and we, therefore, entreat you to hearken with attention, for we are able to speak of things which are to us very great.

When your army entered the country of the Six Nations, we called you "town destroyer;" to this day, when your name is heard, our women look behind them and turn pale, and our children cling close to the necks of their mothers.

When our chiefs returned from Fort Stanwix, and laid before our council what had been done there, our nation was surprised to hear how great a country you had compelled them to give up to you, without your paying to us anything for it. Everyone said that your hearts were yet swelled with resentment against us for what had happened during the war, but that one day you would consider it with more kindness. We asked each other, *"What have we done to deserve such severe chastisement?"*

Father. When you kindled your thirteen fires separately, the wise men assembled at them told us that you were all brothers, the children of one great father, who regarded the red people as his children. They called us brothers, and invited us to his protection. They told us that he resided beyond the great water

Cornplanter. From Thomas L. McKenney and James Hall, History of the Indian Tribes of North America *(Philadelphia, 1863–64). Smithsonian Institution, National Anthropological Archives.*

where the sun first rises, and that he was a king whose power no people could resist, and that his goodness was as bright as the sun. What they said went to our hearts. We accepted the invitation, and promised to obey him. What the Seneca nation promises, they faithfully perform. When you refused obedience to that king, he commanded us to assist his beloved men in making you sober. In obeying him, we did no more than yourselves had led us to promise. We were deceived, but your people teaching us to confide in that king, had helped to deceive us, and we now appeal to your breast. Is all the blame ours?

Father. When we saw that we had been deceived, and heard the invitation which you gave us to draw near to the fire you had kindled, and talk with you concerning peace, we made haste towards it. You told us you could crush us to nothing, and you demanded from us a great country, as the price of that peace which you had offered to us, *as if our want of strength had destroyed our rights.* Our chiefs had felt your power, and were unable to contend against you, and they therefore gave up that country. What they agreed to has bound our nation, but your anger against us must by this time be cooled, and although our strength is not increased, nor your power become less, we ask you to consider calmly—*were the terms dictated to us by your commissioners reasonable and just?*

Father. You have said that we were in your hand, and that by closing it you could crush us to nothing. Are you determined to crush us? If you are, tell us so, that those of our nation who have become your children, and have determined to die so, may know what to do. In this case, one chief has said, he would ask you to put him out of his pain. Another, who will not think of dying by the hand of his father, has said he will retire to eat of the fatal root, * and sleep with his fathers in peace.

All the land we have been speaking of belonged to the Six Nations. No part of it ever belonged to the king of England, and he could not give it to you.

Hear us once more. At Fort Stanwix we agreed to deliver up those of our people who should do you any wrong, and that you might try them and punish them according to your law. We delivered up two men accordingly. But instead of trying them according to your law, the lowest of your people took them from your magistrate, and put them immediately to death. It is just to punish the murder with death, but the Senecas will not deliver up their people to men who disregard the treaties of their own nation.

*Probably the root of the May apple, a poisonous root used by Indians to commit suicide.

Joseph Brant. From McKenney and Hall, History of the Indian Tribes of North America *(1836–44). Smithsonian Institution, National Anthropological Archives.*

1794

Joseph Brant (Thayendanegea, "He Places Together Two Bets"), the eloquent Mohawk orator and powerful war chief of the Six Nations, had played a significant role in Indian-white relations throughout the Revolutionary War. As at home in British drawing rooms and with American colonists as he was in Indian villages, he could deal equally well with all three groups.

His sympathies were with the British cause, however, and after the war ended he and his followers settled in Canada, along the Grand River near Brantford, Ontario. Brant continued his efforts to establish a permanent peace among the Indians, the British, and the newly established government of the United States.

At a council meeting of Indians and whites held at the Onondaga village on Buffalo Creek, New York, on 21 April, Brant once again appealed to the honor of both the British and the Americans, explaining why the peace terms and territorial boundaries they had previously proposed were unsatisfactory.

Addressing himself directly to Colonel John Butler, who represented George III, and to General Israel Chapin, who represented the government of the United States, Brant assured them that if they were honest in their dealings with the Indians, the latter, as independent people, would respect the terms that they all agreed upon.

> Brother. The answer you have brought us is not according [to] what we expected, which was the reason for our long delay: the business would have been done with expedition had the United States agreed to our proposals. We would then have collected our associates, and repaired to Venango [in Pennsylvania], the place you proposed for meeting us.
>
> Brother. It is not now in our power to accept your invitation, provided we were to go, you would conduct the business, as you might think proper, this has been the case at all the treaties held from time to time, by your commissioners. . . .
>
> Brother. We, the Six Nations, have been exerting ourselves to keep peace since the conclusion of the war. We think it would be best for both parties, we advised the confederate nations to request a meeting, about half way between us and the United States, in order that such steps might be taken as would bring about a peace; this request was made, and Congress appointed commissioners to meet us at Muskingum, which we agreed to, a boundary line was then proposed by us, and refused by Governor St. Clair,* one of your commissioners. The Wyandots, a few Delawares, and some others met the commissioners, though not authorized, and confirmed the lines of what was not their property, but common to all nations. . . .
>
> Brother. Our proposals have not met with the success from Congress that we expected; this still leaves us in a similar situation to what we were when we first entered on the business.
>
> Brother. You must recollect the number of chiefs who have, at divers times, waited on Congress; they have pointed out the means to be taken, and held out the same language, uniformly, at one time as another, that was, if you would withdraw your claim to the boundary line, and lands within the line, as offered by us. Had this been done, peace would have taken place, and, unless this still be done, we see no other method of accomplishing it.
>
> Brother. We have borne everything patiently for this long time

past, we have done everything we could consistently do with the welfare of our nations in general—notwithstanding the many advantages that have been taken of us, by individuals making purchases from us, the Six Nations, whose fraudulent conduct toward us Congress has never taken notice of, nor in any wise [way] seen us rectified, nor made our minds easy. This is the case to the present day; our patience is now entirely worn out; you see the difficulties we labor under, so that we cannot at present rise from our seats and attend your council at Venango, agreeable to your invitation. The boundary line we pointed out we think a just one, although the United States claims lands west of that line; the trifle that has been paid by the United States can be no object in comparison to what a peace would be.

Brother. We are of the same opinion with the people of the United States—you consider yourselves as independent people, we, as the original inhabitants of this country, and sovereigns of the soil, look upon ourselves as equally independent, and free as any other nation or nations. This country was given to us by the Great Spirit above; we wish to enjoy it, and have our passage [a]long the lake, within the line we have pointed out.

Brother. The great exertions we have made, for this number of years, to accomplish a peace, and have not been able to obtain it, our patience, as we have already observed, is exhausted, and we are discouraged from persevering any longer. We therefore throw ourselves under the protection of the Great Spirit above, who, we hope, will order all things for the best. We have told you our patience is worn out, but not so far but that we wish for peace, and whenever we hear that pleasing sound, we shall pay atten-tion to it.

---

*General Arthur St. Clair, the governor of the Northwest Territory, was the principal negotiator. Negotiators at treaty councils, appointed by the American government, were called "commissioners."

1794

Little Turtle (Michikinikwa), the Miami chief, was an intrepid fighter. In 1790 he had successfully repulsed both Kentucky militiamen and the U.S. Army in Ohio. However, just before his final, disastrous battle at Fallen Timbers, Ohio, against General "Mad Anthony" Wayne, he had a change of heart, and advised seeking peace. The night before the fight, he expressed his reasons at a council meeting of the Miamis.

We have beaten the enemy twice under separate commanders. We cannot expect the same good fortune always to attend us. The Americans are now led by a chief who never sleeps: The night and the day are alike to him. And during all the time that he has been marching upon our villages, notwithstanding the watchfulness of our young men, we have never been able to surprise him. Think well of it. There is something whispers me, it would be prudent to listen to his offers of peace.

Little Turtle. A lithograph from a painting attributed to Gilbert Stuart (1797). Smithsonian Institution, National Anthropological Archives.

4

The 19th Century
"I never called a white man
a dog . . ."

During the 19th century, two inventions, the daguerreotype (1839) and the camera (1840), made possible a less "romanticized" and more realistic visual record of American Indian life. They eliminated the hitherto mutually exclusive myths of the Indian as a "noble savage" and as an unregenerate barbarian. What emerged was the picture of the American Indian as a human being.

From the Louisiana Purchase of 1803 to the Alaska Purchase of 1867, the United States annexed continental North American lands through purchase and treaties with foreign powers and the Indians, until almost all of the continent north of the Rio Grande and south of the Canadian border was part of the United States. Transcontinental railroads cut through Indian boundaries, in direct violation of Thomas Jefferson's earlier promises that the lands west of the Mississippi would remain Indian territory. Many tribes were greatly reduced in number as a result of sickness and continual warfare, and those remaining were often forced to relocate on isolated, inhospitable, often desolate reservations. Those who tried to escape were captured and forcibly resettled. Suppression of traditional customs and restrictive control of both individual Indians and entire tribes were the rule.

 In 1830, by order of President Andrew Jackson, the Five Civilized Tribes (Creek, Catawba, Cherokee, Chickasaw, and Choctaw, so called because of their quick adoption of white ways, including farming, slavery, living in brick houses, seminary education, and the publication, by the Cherokees, of a bilingual newspaper) were forced to take the "Trail of Tears" (Nuna-da-ut-sun'y, "the trail where they cried"), the thousand-mile, ten-year trek from their homes in Georgia to Indian Territory west of the Mississippi set aside for them by government decree, during which one-quarter of the tribal population died of hunger, disease, and hardship. The Cherokees, who had kept to the terms of every treaty, knew that they were being cruelly used. From their capital at New Echota, Georgia, they sent a memorial to the Congress, accusing the United States of planning genocide.

The same divisiveness that had destroyed the Iroquois Confederacy now threatened the Cherokees. Missionary-educated John Ross advocated moving as the only road to survival; others, like John Ridge, argued for remaining on original Cherokee lands and keeping the traditional ways. Their arguments were printed side by side in the bilingual Cherokee *Phoenix*. Attempts on the part of the U.S. government, pursuing this same policy of enforced migration, to make the Seminoles of Florida leave the Southeast, led to a war. The Indians' resistance was weakened by the imprisonment and subsequent death of their young chief, Osceola, in 1837. They surrendered altogether in 1842 and were moved westward to Oklahoma.

All over the country, Indian leaders fought to free their people from the domination and alien values of the white man. American Indian prophets, orators, and chiefs protested strongly, their words remaining as a permanent record of the Indians' resistance to the whites' inhumanity. The Indians were fully aware of the wrongs being done to them, though they were rarely able to secure redress.

Messianic movements, aiming to restore the traditional Indian way of life, had arisen periodically since the days of Deganawidah, the 16th-century Iroquois prophet, who, with Hiawatha, founded the Iroquois Confederacy. During the 19th century, such prophets frequently led rebellions against the white man. In Washington and Oregon, Smoholla (Smoqula, "The Preacher"), a Wanapum Indian, claimed, after his conversion to Christianity, to have had visions, and to have gone on a trip to the spirit world. When he "returned" he told his people that he had a message from "the other side." Only by rejecting the white men's culture and values, he said, and returning to their own traditional values, could the Indians regain the land they had lost, and make the whites disappear. The Dreamer religion, which he founded, combined Catholicism and the "Ghost Dance" of another messianic religion. The congregation sang songs and danced simple dances to the accompaniment of drums. They also practiced confession, and reported their dreams at the services Smoholla held on Sundays (he had visited a Catholic mission as a boy, and probably absorbed some of its practices). He preached that Indian land should not be plowed or sold. Smoholla's teachings inspired such outstanding Indian leaders as Chief Joseph (Hinmaton Yalakit, "Thunder Rolling in the Heights") and his rebellion of 1877, and flourished among Indians of the Northwest until well into the 20th century.

The Ghost Dance, whose rituals the Dreamer religion incorporated, was the best known of these messianic cults. It was founded by Jack Wilson (Wovoka, "The Cutter," also known as Waneika, "One Who Makes Life"). Wilson, a Paiute prophet, claimed that during an eclipse of the sun (1 January 1889) he had had a vision in which he received a message from God, instructing him to journey from tribe to tribe and teach a new way of life and a new doctrine to the Indians. They were to give up European—now American—ways, return to the old customs practiced before the Europeans arrived, and to the simple life, with no guns, no alcohol, and no trade goods. And, if the Indians performed the Ghost Dance, the religion's chief ritual, the whites would disappear, the land would be returned to the Indian people, and all the great warriors of former times would come back to earth. This revitalization movement became known as the Ghost Dance religion, and many Indians stopped fighting, laid down their arms in obedience to its pacifist tenets, and danced the slow, hypnotic dance instead. Some even wore shirts called Ghost shirts, which were supposed to protect them against bullets. Particularly appealing was Wilson's further promise that all Indians who followed his teachings would eventually be reunited on earth, in a world free from death, disease, and misery.

Attempts to suppress the Ghost Dance led to the murder of Chief Sitting Bull (Tatanka Iotake) and to the tragic massacre of the Sioux at Wounded Knee, South Dakota, in 1890, events which marked a last desperate effort by Indians to counteract the demoralization brought about by white men's efforts to force them to conform to the European way of life, and to give up hunting for farming.

The eloquent, forceful oratory that had always been a basic part of Indian communication began, in the 19th century, to achieve national recognition in North America. Indian chiefs and official orators addressed not only their own tribal brothers and members of allied and hostile tribes, but government officials as well, both at formal treaty meetings and on other occasions in America and Europe. In 1818 a group of Iroquois went to Europe, and for five years (1839–45) George Catlin, a traveler and artist who painted many scenes of Indian life, toured the Old World with a large group of Ojibwas and Iowas.

Beginning with Thomas Jefferson, presidents of the United States invited Indian delegations to Washington, D.C., to talk with government officials, and with the presidents themselves. They spoke on their own behalf, directly, as well as through official interpreters, although the latter, as so often in the past, sometimes disguised, distorted, or misrepresented what had been said in the language of the Indians. These Indians came hoping to regain their land; the government hoped to force them off it.

Throughout the century, intratribal conflicts arose between those who wanted to maintain their old ways and those who were willing to try their luck as farmers, as the United States government wanted them to. Newly created government bureaus attempted first to kill off the Indians; then to incorporate them into the mainstream of society, on the white man's terms. In 1830 there was a hopeful development when the Supreme Court recognized the Indian tribes as sovereign nations with the right to govern their own internal affairs, and four years later, the Bureau of Indian Affairs was organized as part of the War Department. But on 3 March 1871, Congress enacted legislation declaring that, although treaties made up to that time with individual Indian tribes would continue to be honored, no further treaties or agreements would be negotiated with individual Indian groups. Since that time, government decisions about the Indians, and consequent laws, have been imposed on them from without, by means of congressional acts and executive orders, and frequently without any consultation. In 1880 the government established federal jurisdiction on Indian reservations for specific criminal offenses. In 1887 the Dawes Allotment Act, ignoring the requirements set by the Sioux Treaty of 1868, broke up many of the great Indian reservations. Finally, in 1897, President McKinley declared that Indian governments should be dissolved and that Indian Territory should be made part of the United States, completely eliminating the possibility of separate Indian land and existence.

Perhaps the most significant event, in terms of its meaning for today's American Indians, was the case of *Standing Bear* v. *Crook*, heard in the United States Supreme Court on 8 April 1879. Standing Bear, or Mon-chu-non-zhin, a Ponca Indian, had rejected the order to move his Poncas from their Nebraska reservation to Indian Territory. In spite of his protests, however, he and a group of chiefs were taken south to choose a spot for a reservation. They refused to select a place, and when they got to Arkansas City, Kansas, they asked to be returned to their homes. Refused permission to go back to Nebraska, they escaped on foot with only a little money and a single blanket apiece, and in 40 days walked the 500-mile distance back. They were, however, forced to leave the reservation again and return to Indian Territory. The constant moves from one climate to another caused outbreaks of sickness among the Indians, and within a year a third of the tribe had died. When Standing Bear's son died, he wanted to bury the boy on his original reservation. Accompanied by some of his faithful followers, he took his son's bones and started, once more, for Nebraska. But he got only as far as the Omahas' reservation on the Niobrara River, where he arrived two months later, destitute and starving. They gave him some of their land on which to plant seed, but before he could, the Poncas were arrested by soldiers with orders to return them to Indian Territory.

Arrested and imprisoned, Standing Bear pleaded for the right to live where he chose. General George "Three Star" Crook, who had taken him into custody, spoke with the chief in prison, and was so moved by what he was told about the mistreatment of the Poncas and the way in which their lands had been misappropriated by the whites that he held up orders to return Standing Bear to Indian Territory, while Thomas Henry Tibbles, an Omaha newspaperman, published the story in newspapers across the country. A young Nebraska lawyer, John L. Webster, and Andrew Popple-ton, the chief attorney for the Union Pacific Railroad, volunteered their services to Standing Bear, waiving their right to legal fees. Judge Elmer S. Dundy was brought back from a bear hunt to hear the case.

Standing Bear's lawyers pleaded for his right, as a person, to live wherever he chose. They sued for a writ of habeas corpus (everyone's right as a protection against illegal imprisonment), which was denied by the United States District Attorney on the ground that Indians were "not persons within the meaning of the law." Given an opportunity to speak for himself, Standing Bear pleaded passionately for fair treatment. He persuaded Judge Dundy to rule that an Indian *was* a "person" within the meaning of the habeas corpus act, and that Indians, in time of peace, could live where they pleased, and could not be forcibly transported or confined on any particular reservation against their will. After the verdict was announced, the spectators gave it a thunderous, standing ovation.

Those Poncas who were still in Indian Territory then sued to be permitted to rejoin Standing Bear and his followers in Omaha. The denial of their petition meant that the already small tribe would be split still further. Standing Bear's band lived as free men in the north, but the Poncas in Indian Territory were forced to remain there, virtual prisoners of the reservation policy.

But Standing Bear had won a significant victory, and an important precedent had been set for future civil rights actions on the part of the Indians. The Indian was, henceforth, a "person" under the law.

Red Jacket, wearing the coat whose color gave him his English name, and a medal presented to him by George Washington. From McKenney and Hall, History of the Indian Tribes of North America. *Smithsonian Institution, National Anthropological Archives.*

1805

Red Jacket (Sagoyewatha, "He Who Causes Them to Be Awake"), a famous Seneca orator, subchief, and warrior, was unalterably opposed to Christianity. After a Protestant missionary had addressed the tribe at a meeting in Buffalo, New York, Red Jacket replied, contrasting the life of the Indians before and after the coming of the white man. In the matter of the new religion advocated by the missionary, he was skeptical. Before recommending Christianity for his fellow Indians, he said he would wait to see whether it made his white neighbors better neighbors and more honest in their dealings with the Indians.

> Brother, this council fire was kindled by you; it was at your request that we came together at this time; we have listened with attention to what you have said, you have requested us to speak our minds freely; this gives us great joy, for we now consider that we stand upright before you, and can speak what we think; all have heard your voice, and all speak to you as one man, our minds are agreed.
>
> Brother, listen to what we say. There was a time when our forefathers owned this great land. Their seats extended from the rising to the setting sun. The Great Spirit had made it for the use of the Indians. He had created the buffalo, the deer, and other animals for food. He made the bear and the beaver and their

111

skins served us for clothing. He had scattered them over the country, and taught us how to take them. He had caused the earth to produce corn for bread.

All this he had done for His red children because he loved them. If we had any disputes about hunting grounds, they were generally settled without the shedding of much blood.

But an evil day came upon us; your forefathers crossed the great waters, and landed on this island. Their numbers were small, they found friends, and not enemies; they told us they had fled from their own country for fear of wicked men and come here to enjoy their religion. They asked for a small seat, we took pity on them, granted their request, and they gave us poison in return. The white people had now found our country, and more came among us; yet we did not fear them, we took them to be friends, they called us brothers, we believed them and gave them a larger seat. At length their numbers had greatly increased; they wanted more land; they wanted our country. Our eyes were opened; and our minds became uneasy. Wars took place; Indians were hired to fight against Indians, and many of our people were destroyed. They also brought strong liquor among us, it has . . . slain thousands.

Brother, our seats were once large, and yours were very small; you now have become a great people, and we have scarcely a place left to spread our blankets; you have got our country, but are not satisfied, you want to force your religion upon us. . . . We only know what you tell us about it; how shall we know when to believe, being so often deceived by the white people? . . .

Brother, we are told that you have been preaching to white people in this place; these people are our neighbors, we are acquainted with them, we will wait a little while and see what effect your preaching has upon them. If we find it does them good, makes them honest, and less disposed to cheat Indians, we will then consider again what you have said.

Joseph Brant in a more active moment. A portrait by William Berczy. The National Gallery of Canada, Ottawa.

1807

Shortly before his death in 1807, Joseph Brant, the eloquent Mohawk sachem, wrote a letter to an unidentified correspondent in which he analyzed the differences between the Indians' and white man's law, and expressed his contempt for the latter.

> Among us we have no prisons, we have no pompous parade of courts; we have no written laws, and yet judges are revered among us as they are among you, and their decisions are as highly regarded.
>
> Property, to say the least, is well guarded, and crimes are as impartially punished. We have among us no splendid villains above the control of our laws. Daring wickedness is never suffered to triumph over helpless innocence. The estates of widows and orphans are never devoured by enterprising sharpers. In a word, we have no robbery under color of law.

113

1810

Tecumseh (Tecumtha, "One Who Passes Across Intervening Space From One Point To Another"), Shawnee orator and warrior, vehemently opposed the encroachment of whites on Indian territory. Without his knowledge, some individual Shawnees ceded lands to the American government under the terms of the Treaty of Fort Wayne (1809), and at a meeting in Vincennes, Indiana on 12 August, Tecumseh protested to General William H. Harrison, governor of the Indiana Territory, who had been present at the signing of the treaty, against what he considered the illegal purchase of this land.

It is true I am a Shawnee. My forefathers were warriors. Their son is a warrior. From them I only take my existence; from my tribe I take nothing. I am the maker of my own fortune; and oh! that I could make that of my red people, and of my country, as great as the conceptions of my mind, when I think of the Spirit that rules the universe. I would not then come to Governor Harrison, to ask him to tear the treaty, and to obliterate the landmark; but I would say to him, "Sir, you have liberty to return to your own country." The being within, communing with past ages, tells me, that once, nor until lately, there was no white man on this continent. That it then all belonged to red men, children of the same parents, placed on it by the Great Spirit that made them, to keep it, to traverse it, to enjoy its productions, and to fill it with the same race. Once a happy race. Since made miserable by the white people, who are never contented, but always encroaching. The way, and the only way to check and stop this evil, is, for all the red men to unite in claiming a common and equal right in the land, as it was at first, and should be yet; for it never was divided, but belongs to all, for the use of each. That no part has a right to sell, even to each other, much less to strangers, those who want all, and will not do with less. The white people have no right to take the land from the Indians, because they had it first; it is theirs. They may sell, but all must join. Any sale not made by all is not valid. The late sale is bad. It was made by a part only. Part do not know how to sell. It requires all to make a bargain for all. All red men have equal rights to the unoccupied land. The right of occupancy is as good in one place as in another. There cannot be two occupations in the same place. The first excludes all others. It is not so in hunting or traveling; for there the same ground will serve many, as they may follow each other all day; but the camp is stationary, and that is occupancy. It belongs to the first who sits down on his blanket or skins, which he has thrown upon the ground and till he leaves it no other has a right [to it].

Tecumseh. From Benson J. Lossing, The Pictorial Field-Book of the War of 1812 *(New York, 1869). Copy after a pencil sketch by Pierre Le Dru (ca. 1808). Smithsonian Institution, National Anthropological Archives.*

Petalesharo (Pitalescharu, "Man Chief"), handsome principal chief of the
Skidi Pawnees, had a colorful career, and was greatly admired by both
Indians and whites. He was the guest of President James Monroe and
Secretary of War John C. Calhoun in Washington, D.C. from October
1821 to March 1822. At a conference held in February, President Monroe
urged the chief to sign a pact guaranteeing peace and friendship between the
Pawnees and the United States. In his reply, made on 4 February,
Petalesharo indicated a desire for peace, but seemed to feel that many of the
problems had arisen because of the basic incompatibility of the white way of
life and that of the Indian.

> My Great Father . . . The Great Spirit made us all—he made my
> skin red, and yours white, he placed us on this earth, and
> intended that we should live differently from each other.
>
> He made the whites to cultivate the earth, and feed on
> domestic animals, but he made us, redskins, to rove through the
> uncultivated woods and plains, to feed on wild animals, and to
> dress with their skins. He also intended that we should go to war,
> to take scalps, steal horses from and triumph over our enemies,
> cultivate peace at home, and promote the happiness of each
> other. I believe there are no people of my color on this earth who
> do not believe in the Great Spirit—in rewards and punishments.
> We worship him, but we worship him not as you do. We differ
> from you in appearance and manners as well as in our customs,
> and we differ from you in our religion; we have no large houses as
> you have to worship the Great Spirit in; if we had them today, we
> would want others tomorrow, for we have not, like you, a fixed
> habitation—we have no settled home except our villages, where
> we remain but two moons in twelve. We, like animals, rove
> through the country, whilst you whites reside between us and
> heaven; but still, my Great Father, we love the Great Spirit—we
> acknowledge his supreme power—our peace, our health, and our
> happiness depend upon him, and our lives belong to him—he
> made us and he can destroy us.
>
> My Great Father. Some of your good chiefs [missionaries], as
> they are called, have proposed to send some of their good people
> among us to change our habits, to make us work and live like the
> white people. I will not tell a lie—I am going to tell the truth.
> You love your country, you love your people, you love the
> manner in which they live, and you think your people brave. I
> am like you, my Great Father, I love my country, I love my
> people, I love the manner in which they live, and think myself
> and warriors brave. Spare me then, Father, let me enjoy my
> country, and pursue the buffalo, and the beaver, and the other

Petalesharo. A painting copied from an original portrait by Charles Bird King (ca. 1821 or 1822). Smithsonian Institution, National Anthropological Archives.

wild animals of our country, and I will trade their skins with your people. I have grown up and lived thus long without work—I am in hopes you will suffer me to die without it. We have plenty of buffalo, deer, and other wild animals—we have also an abundance of horses. We have everything we want, we have plenty of land, if you will keep your people off of it. . . .

It is too soon, my Great Father, to send those good men among us. We are not starving yet—we wish you to permit us to enjoy the chase until the game of our country is exhausted, until the wild animals have become extinct. Let us exhaust our present resources before you make us toil and interrupt our happiness—let me continue to live as I have done, and after I have passed to the good or evil spirit from off the wilderness of my present life, the subsistence of my children may become so precarious as to need and embrace the assistance of those good people.

There was a time when we did not know the whites—our wants then were fewer than they are now. They were always within our control—we had then seen nothing which we could not get. Before our intercourse with the whites (who have caused such a destruction in our game), we could lie down and sleep, and when we awoke we would find the buffalo feeding around our camp—but now we are killing them for their skins, and feeding the wolves with their flesh, to make our children cry over their bones. . . .

1832

When forced to abandon his village at Rock Island, Illinois, in 1831, Black Hawk (Ma-Ka-tai-me-she-Kia-Kiak, "Black Sparrow Hawk"), a famous Sauk chief, crossed the Mississippi with his people. They settled in Iowa on the other shore. When he attempted to return to Rock Island in the spring of 1832, he was pursued and attacked by the Illinois militia. Finally cornered at the mouth of the Bad Axe River, and fired on by land forces and from a riverboat, he saw his people, including women and children, killed where they stood, even though they had waved a white flag. Black Hawk escaped, but in May, he surrendered to Zachary Taylor at Prairie du Chien in Crawford County, Wisconsin, and was imprisoned and shackled at Jefferson Barracks in St. Louis. He denounced his captors thus:

You have taken me prisoner with all my warriors. I am much grieved, for I expected, if I did not defeat you, to hold out much longer, and give you more trouble before I surrendered. I tried hard to bring you into ambush, but your last general understands Indian fighting. The first one was not so wise. When I saw that I could not beat you by Indian fighting, I determined to rush on you, and fight you face to face. I fought hard. But your guns were well aimed. The bullets flew like birds in the air, and whizzed by our ears like the wind through the trees in the winter. My warriors fell around me; it began to look dismal. I saw my evil day at hand. The sun rose dim on us in the morning, and at night it sunk in a dark cloud, and looked like a ball of fire. That was the last sun that shone on Black Hawk. His heart is dead, and no longer beats quick in his bosom. He is now a prisoner to the white men; they will do with him as they wish. But he can stand torture, and is not afraid of death. He is no coward. Black Hawk is an Indian.

He has done nothing for which an Indian ought to be ashamed. He has fought for his countrymen, the squaws and papooses, against white men, who came, year after year, to cheat them and take away their lands. You know the cause of our making war. It is known to all white men. They ought to be ashamed of it. The white men despise the Indians, and drive them from their homes. But the Indians are not deceitful. The white men speak bad of the Indian, and look at him spitefully. But the Indian does not tell lies; Indians do not steal.

An Indian who is as bad as the white men could not live in our nation; he would be put to death, and eaten up by the wolves. The white men are bad schoolmasters; they carry false looks, and deal in false actions; they smile in the face of the poor Indian to cheat him; they shake them by the hand to gain their confidence, to make them drunk, to deceive them, and ruin our wives. We

Black Hawk. George Catlin's undated portrait reveals the brooding pride of this famous chief. Smithsonian Institution, National Portrait Gallery.

told them to let us alone, but they followed on and beset our paths, and they coiled themselves among us like the snake. They poisoned us by their touch. We were not safe. We lived in danger. We were becoming like them, hypocrites and liars, adulterers, lazy drones, all talkers, and no workers.

We looked up to the Great Spirit. We went to our great father [President Andrew Jackson]. We were encouraged. His great council gave us fair words and big promises, but we got no satisfaction. Things were growing worse. There were no deer in the forest. The opossum and beaver were fled, the springs were drying up, and our squaws and papooses without victuals to keep them from starving; we called a great council and built a large fire. The spirit of our fathers arose and spoke to us to avenge our wrongs or die. . . . We set up the war whoop, and dug up the tomahawk; our knives were ready, and the heart of Black Hawk swelled high in his bosom when he led his warriors to battle. He is satisfied. He will go to the world of spirits contented. He has done his duty. His father will meet him there, and commend him.

Black Hawk is a true Indian, and disdains to cry like a woman. He feels for his wife, his children and friends. But he does not care for himself. He cares for his nation and the Indians. They will suffer. He laments their fate. The white men do not scalp the head, but they do worse—they poison the heart, it is not pure with them. His countrymen will not be scalped, but they will, in a few years, become like the white men, so that you can't trust them, and there must be, as in the white settlements, nearly as many officers as men, to take care of them and keep them in order.

Farewell, my nation. Black Hawk tried to save you, and avenge your wrongs. He drank the blood of some of the whites. He has been taken prisoner, and his plans are stopped. He can do no more. He is near his end. His sun is setting, and he will rise no more. Farewell to Black Hawk.

1837

The outstanding Mandan chief, The Four Bears (Ma-to-pe), had always been friendly to the whites. But while recovering from an attack of smallpox, he had to watch his entire family and many of his people sicken and die in agony from this terrible disfiguring disease that had been introduced among the Indians by his erstwhile friends. Finally, he could bear it no longer. Ignoring all pleas, he went out to a hill near his village, determined to starve himself to death to protest the perfidy of the whites in breaking their many promises and spreading disease. At the end of six days,

The Four Bears. From Maximilian, Prince zu Wied-Nuwied Travels *(1843), pl. 13. An engraving from a painting by Karl Bodmer (1834). Smithsonian Institution, National Anthropological Archives.*

he dragged himself back, and exhorted his people to avenge the wrongs that had been done to them by the whites.

My Friends, one and all, listen to what I have to say. . . . I have loved the whites. I have lived with them . . . and to the best of my knowledge I have always protected them from the insults of others, which they cannot deny. The Four Bears never saw a white man hungry but what he gave him to eat, drink, and a buffalo skin to sleep on, in time of need. I was always ready to die for them, which they cannot deny. I have done everything that a redskin could do for them, and how they have repaid it! With ingratitude. I have never called a white man a dog, but today, I do pronounce them to be a set of black-hearted dogs. They have deceived me, them that I always considered as brothers turned out to be my worst enemies. I have been in many battles, and often wounded, but the wounds of my enemies I exult in. But today I am wounded, and by whom? By those same white dogs that I have always considered and treated as brothers. I do not fear death, my friends. You know it. But to die with my face rotten, that even the wolves will shrink with horror at seeing me, and say to themselves, "That is Four Bears, the friend of the whites."

Listen well to what I have to say, as it will be the last time you will hear me. Think of your wives, children, brothers, sisters, with their faces all rotten, caused by those dogs the whites. Think of all that my friends, and rise all together and not leave one of them alive. The Four Bears will act his part.

(Three days later he was dead.)

In this picture one sees the poverty and degradation feared by Maris Bryant Pierce if the Indians continued to be separated from their lands and traditions. The mothers and children appear hungry, the others confused and discontented as they attempt to deal with an indifferent trader. Reproduced from the Collections of the Library of Congress.

1838

In a period of sixteen years, the Ogden Land Company was able to purchase more than 300,000 acres of land from the Senecas of New York State for fifty cents an acre. It told the Indians that the United States government had ordered them to move, and would punish them severely if they refused, then, in turn, misrepresented the facts to the government. It also bribed individual Indian chiefs to sell land belonging to the tribe. In 1838 the government negotiated a treaty with the tribe, requiring the Senecas to sell *all* their New York lands and move to the Indian Territory west of the Mississippi. The government appropriated $400,000 to carry out the treaty. Many Senecas protested that the treaty was illegal, that the government had used bribery to get signatures from individual members of the tribe, and that only eighteen of the eighty-one members of the Seneca council had ratified it.

Maris Bryant Pierce, an educated Seneca, speaking to the members of the Baptist Church of Buffalo, New York, on 28 August, strongly protested the exploitation of the Senecas by avaricious land speculators, and the forced removal of his people to strange and hostile environments.

> In the first place the white man wants our land; in the next place it is said that the offer for it is liberal; in the next place that we shall be better off to remove from the vicinity of the whites and settle in the neighborhood of our fellow red man, where the woods flock with game, and the streams abound with fishes. . . .
> The fact that the whites want our land imposes no obligation on us to sell it, nor does it hold forth an inducement to do so, unless it leads them to offer a price equal in value to us. We neither know nor feel any debt of gratitude which we owe to them, in consequence of their "loving kindness or tender mercies" toward us, that should cause us to make a sacrifice of our property or our interest, to their wonted avarice and which, like the mother of the horse leech, cries give, give, and is never sated. . . . By what mode of calculation or rules of judgment is one or two dollars a liberal offer to us, when many times that sum would be only fair to the avarice of the land speculator? Since in us is vested a perfect title to the land, I know not why we may not, when we wish, dispose of it at such prices as we may see fit to agree upon. . . .
> "Westward the star of empire takes it away,"* and whenever that empire is held by the white man, nothing is safe or unmolested or enduring against his avidity for gain. . . . Population is with rapid strides going beyond the Mississippi. . . . And in the process of time, will not our territory there be as subject to the wants of the whites as that which we now occupy is? . . . The proximity of our then situation to that of other and more warlike tribes will expose us to constant harassing by them; and not only this, but the character of those worse than Indians, those *white borderers,* who infest, yes infest, the western border of the white population will annoy us more fatally than even the Indians themselves. Surrounded thus by the natives of the soil, and hunted by such a class of whites, who neither "fear God nor regard man," how shall we be better off there than where we are now? . . .
> I need not insult your common sense by endeavoring to show that it is *stupid folly* to suppose that a removal from our present location to the western wilds would improve our condition.

*Pierce is alluding here to a phrase used by John Quincy Adams in his *Oration at Plymouth* (1802), "Westward the star of empire takes its way."

Chief Seattle Historic Photo Collection, Washington State Historical Society.

1855

Chief Seattle (Seathl) of the Suqwamish and Duwamish Indians was the first signatory of the Treaty of Port Elliot, which paved the way for the creation of an Indian reservation there. (Today his descendants are fighting for fishing rights in that same territory, which is now the state of Washington.) In a speech to Isaac Stevens, governor of the Washington Territory, Chief Seattle pleaded for humane treatment of his people and asked the white men to attempt to understand Indian-white differences:

> Yonder sky that has wept tears of compassion upon my people for centuries untold, and which to us appears changeless and eternal, may change. Today is fair. Tomorrow it may be overcast with clouds. My words are like the stars that never change. Whatever Seattle says the great chief at Washington can rely upon with as

much certainty as he can upon the return of the sun or the seasons. The white chief says that the big chief in Washington sends us greetings of friendship and good will. That is kind of him for we know he has little need of our friendship in return. His people are many. They are like the grass that covers vast prairies. My people are few. They resemble the scattering trees of a storm-swept plain. . . . I will not dwell on, or mourn over, our untimely decay, nor reproach our paleface brothers with hastening it, as we too may have been somewhat to blame. . . .

Your God is not our God. Your God loves your people and hates mine. . . . Our God, the Great Spirit, seems . . . to have forsaken us. Your God makes your people strong every day. Soon they will fill the land. Our people are ebbing away like a rapidly receding tide that will never return. The white man's God cannot love our people or He would protect them. They seem to be orphans who can look nowhere for help. How can we then be brothers? We are two distinct races with separate origins and separate destinies. There is little in common between us. . . .

The red man has ever fled the approach of the white man, as the morning mist flees before the morning sun. However your proposition seems fair and I think that my people will accept it and will retire to the reservation you offer them. Then we will dwell apart in peace.

. . . It matters little where we pass the remnants of our days. They will not be many . . . But why should I mourn at the untimely fate of my people? . . . Your time of decay may be distant, but it will surely come, for even the white man, whose God walked and talked with him as friend with friend, cannot be exempt from the common destiny. We may be brothers, after all. We will see. . . .

And when the last red man shall have perished, and the memory of my tribe shall have become a myth among the white men, these shores will swarm with the invisible dead of my tribe, and when our children's children think themselves alone in the field, the store, the shop, upon the highway, or in the silence of the pathless woods, they will not be alone. At night when the streets of your cities and villages are silent and you think them deserted, they will throng with the returning hosts that once filled and still love this beautiful land. The white man will never be alone.

Let him be just and deal kindly with my people, for the dead are not powerless. Dead, did I say? There is no death, only a change of worlds.

John Ross. *From McKenney and Hall,* History of the Indian Tribes of North America. *Smithsonian Institution, National Anthropological Archives.*

1861

John Ross (Chooweescoowee, "The Egret"), a chief of the Cherokee Nation and called by someone "the bright star of the Cherokees," worked tirelessly to achieve tribal unity. At the Cherokee National Assembly held at Tahlequah (now in Oklahoma), on 9 October, he explained why neutrality was no longer the tribe's most advantageous course of action, and advised them to join with the Confederacy in the Civil War.

Friends and fellow citizens.

. . . At the beginning of the conflict, I felt that the interests of the Cherokee people would be best maintained by remaining quiet and not involving themselves in it prematurely. Our relations had long existed with the United States government and bound us to observe amity and peace alike with all the states. Neutrality was proper and wise so long as there remained a reasonable probability that the difficulty between the two sections of the Union would be settled, as a different course would have placed all our rights in jeopardy and might have led to the sacrifice of the people.

But when there was no longer any reason to believe that the union of the states would be continued, there was no cause to hesitate as to the course the Cherokee Nation should pursue. Our geographical position and domestic institutions allied us to the South, while the developments daily made in our vicinity and as

127

to the purposes of the war waged against the Confederate states clearly pointed out the path of interest. These considerations produced a unanimity of sentiment among the people as to the policy to be adopted by the Cherokee Nation. . . .

. . . to be ready as far as practicable to meet any emergency that might spring upon our northern border, it was thought proper to raise a regiment of mounted men and tender its service to [Confederate] General [Benjamin] McCulloch. . . .

. . . it is believed the regiment will be found as efficient as any other like number of men. It is now in the service of the Confederate states for the purpose of aiding in defending their homes and the common rights of the Indian nations about us. . . .

In long years past, our ancestors met undaunted those who would invade their mountain homes beyond the Mississippi; let not their descendants of the present day be found unworthy of them, or unable to stand by the chivalrous men of the South by whose side they may be called to fight in self-defense.

The Cherokee people do not desire to be involved in war, but self-preservation fully justifies them in the course they have adopted, and they will be recreant to themselves if they do not sustain it to the utmost of their humble abilities.

A treaty with the Confederate states has been entered into and is now submitted for your ratification. In view of the circumstances by which we are surrounded, and the provisions of the treaty, it will be found to be the most important ever negotiated on behalf of the Cherokee Nation, and will mark a new era in its history.

The relations of the Cherokee Nation are changed from the United to the Confederate states, with guarantees of protection. . . . The jurisdiction of the Cherokee courts over all members of the Nation, whether by birth, marriage, or adoption is recognized.

Our title to our lands is placed beyond dispute. Our relations with the Confederate states is that of a ward; theirs to us that of a protectorate with powers restricted. . . .

The Cherokee people stand upon new ground. Let us hope that we shall prosper as we have never done before. New avenues of usefulness and distinction will be opened to the ingenuous youth of the country. Our rights of self government will be more fully recognized, and our citizens be no longer dragged off upon flimsy pretexts to be imprisoned and tried before distant tribunals. No just cause exists for domestic difficulties. Let them be buried with the past and only mutual friendship and harmony be cherished. . . .

Big Eagle. *Sketch by Jack D. Howland, from* Harper's Weekly *(5 October 1867). Smithsonian Institution, National Anthropological Archives.*

1862

To the Santee Sioux, reservation life was another example of the way in which the white men cheated them. In August, Little Crow (Ta-oya-te-duta) led them in an unsuccessful attempt to kill all the whites in the Sioux territory in Minnesota. The Sioux were driven out of Minnesota, and eventually thirty-eight of them were hanged en masse. One of the chiefs who participated in this abortive uprising, but escaped death, was Big Eagle (Wam-di-tan-ka), who many years later recorded his own reactions to the event and the causes that led up to it.

Of the causes that led to the outbreak of August, 1862, much has been said. . . . There was great dissatisfaction among the Indians over many things the whites did . . . the whites were always trying to make the Indians give up their life and live like white men—to go farming, work hard and do as they did—and the Indians did not know how to do that, and did not want to anyway. The Indians wanted to live as they did before the Treaty of Traverse des Sioux—go where they pleased and when they pleased, hunt game wherever they could find it, sell their furs to the traders, and live as they could.

The Indians did not think the traders had done right. The Indians bought goods of them on credit and when the government payments came the traders were on hand with their books, which showed that the Indians owed so much and so much, and as the Indians kept no books they could not deny their accounts, but had to pay them, and sometimes the traders got all their money. I do not say that the traders always cheated and lied about these accounts, but since I have been a citizen I know that many white men, when they go to pay their accounts, often think them too large and refuse to pay them, and they go to law about them and there is much bad feeling. The Indians could not go to law, but there was always trouble over their credits. Under

129

the treaty of Traverse des Sioux the Indians had to pay a very large sum of money to the traders for old debts, some of which ran back fifteen years, and many of those who had got the goods were dead and others were not present, and the traders' books had to be received as to the amounts, and the money was taken from the tribe to pay them. . . .

Then many of the white men often abused the Indians and treated them unkindly. . . . Many of the whites always seemed to say by their manner when they saw an Indian, "I am much better than you," and the Indians did not like this. . . .

All these things made many Indians dislike the whites. . . .

It began to be whispered about that now would be a good time to go to war with the whites and get back the lands. . . . It was also thought that a war with the whites would cause the Sioux to forget the troubles among themselves and enable many of them to pay off some old scores. Though I took part in the war, I was against it. I knew there was no good cause for it, and I had been to Washington and knew the power of the whites and that they would finally conquer us. . . .

But after the first talk of war the counsels of the peace Indians prevailed, and many of us thought the danger had all blown over. There was another thing that helped to stop the war talk. The crops that had been put in by the "farmer" Indians were looking well. . . . It seemed as if the white man's way was certainly the best. . . .

At last the time for the payment came and the Indians came in to the agencies to get their money. But the paymaster did not come. . . . Somebody told the Indians that the payment would never be made. . . .

Of course you know how the battle was fought. The Indians that were in the fight did well, but hundreds of our men did not get into it and did not fire a shot. . . . The whites drove our men out of the ravine by a charge and that ended the battle. . . .

Soon after the battle, I, with many others who had taken part in the war, surrendered to General Sibley Robinson and the other half-breeds assured us that if we would do this we would only be held as prisoners of war a short time, but as soon as I surrendered I was thrown into prison . . . tried and served three years in the prison at Davenport [Iowa] and the penitentiary at Rock Island [Illinois] for taking part in the war. . . . If I had known that I would be sent to the penitentiary I would not have surrendered. . . . I surrendered in good faith, knowing that many of the whites were acquainted with me and that I had not been a murderer, or present when a murder had been committed, and if I had killed or wounded a man it had been in fair open fight. But all feeling on my part about this has long since passed away. . . .

Satanta. Photograph by William S. Soule (ca. 1870). Smithsonian Institution, National Anthropological Archives.

1867

In an effort to control the hostile Indians who were blocking construction of a railroad along the Smoky Hill River in Kansas, General William T. Sherman invited chiefs of the Cheyennes, Arapahos, Kiowas, Comanches, and Prairie Apaches to a peace council he had organized at Medicine Lodge Creek, sixty miles south of Fort Larned. Thousands of Indian warriors, in full regalia, attended the council. For more than a week, they pleaded with Sherman and the other government peace commissioners for peaceful coexistence, asking only that they be permitted to remain in their homes, and to hunt and live as they always had.

A number of chiefs spoke on behalf of their tribes, among them Satanta (Set-tainte, "White Bear") one of the major Kiowa leaders. At first, Satanta refused to sign a treaty that would require, as this one would, that his people give up their way of life, but at last he capitulated, as did the other Indians, to avoid the extinction of his tribe as threatened by General George A. Custer. Under the terms of the agreement that was finally signed, the Kiowas ceded their lands in the valleys of the Arkansas River and the Canadian River (in Indian Territory) to the whites, and agreed to abandon their nomadic life and to move to a reservation in the area which they would share with the Cheyennes, the Comanches, and the Arapahos. The Indians also agreed to withdraw all opposition to the construction of the railroad.

Before he finally gave way, Satanta delivered an impassioned plea for freedom to the commissioners, heard by 5,000 assembled Indians. His remarks were widely quoted in the press.

> You, the commissioners, have come from afar to listen to our grievances. . . . The Kiowas and Comanches have not been fighting . . .
>
> . . . Two years ago I made peace with generals [William S.] Harney and [John B.] Sanborn and Colonel Leavenworth at the mouth of the Little Arkansas.
>
> That peace I have never broken. All the chiefs of the Kiowas, Comanches, and Arapahos are here today; they have come to listen to good words. We have been waiting here a long time to see you and are getting tired. All the land south of Arkansas belongs to the Kiowas and Comanches, and I don't want to give away any of it. I love the land and the buffalo and will not part with it. I want you to understand well what I say. Write it on paper. Let the Great Father see it, and let me hear what he has to say. I want you to understand, also, that the Kiowas and Comanches don't want to fight, and have not been fighting since we made the treaty. I hear a great deal of good talk from the gentlemen whom the Great Father [the President] sends us, but they never do what they say. I don't want any of the medicine lodges [schools and churches] within the country. I want the children raised as I was. When I make peace, it is a long and lasting one—there is no end to it. . . .
>
> . . . I have heard that you intend to settle us on a reservation near the mountains. I don't want to settle. I love to roam over the prairies. There I feel free and happy, but when we settle down we grow pale and die.

Ten Bears speaking at Medicine Lodge Creek. Sketch by Jack D. Howland, from Harper's Weekly, *(ca. October 1867). The Research Libraries, NYPL.*

1867

Like Satanta, the Yamparethka Comanche chief Ten Bears (Parra-wa-samen) spoke to the assembled Indians and government commissioners at a Medicine Lodge Creek treaty council. His speech, a masterpiece of Indian oratory, was at once a moving plea for peace, an accusation of perfidy, and a lyrical paean to the beauty of the country and the life he was being forced to abandon.

> My heart is filled with joy, when I see you here, as the brooks fill with water, when the snows melt in the spring, and I feel glad, as the ponies do when the fresh grass starts in the beginning of the year. I heard of your coming, when I was many sleeps away, and I made but few camps before I met you. I knew that you had come to do good to me and to my people. I looked for the benefits, which would last forever, and so my face shines with joy, as I look upon you. My people have never first drawn a bow or fired a gun against the whites. There has been trouble on the line between us, and my young men have danced the war dance. But it was not begun by us.
>
> It was you who sent out the first soldier, and it was we who sent out the second. Two years ago, I came up upon this road, following the buffalo, that my wives and children might have their cheeks plump, and their bodies warm. But the soldiers fired on us, and since that time there has been a noise, like that of a thunderstorm, and we have not known which way to go. So it was upon the Canadian [border]. Nor have we been made to cry once alone. The blue-dressed soldiers and the Utes came from out of the night, when it was dark and still, and for campfires, they lit our lodges. Instead of hunting game, they killed my

braves and the warriors of the tribe cut short their hair for the dead. So it was in Texas. They made sorrow come into our camps, and we went out like the buffalo bulls, when the cows are attacked. When we found them we killed them, and their scalps hang in our lodges.

The Comanches are not weak and blind, like the pups of a dog when seven sleeps old. They are strong and farsighted, like grown horses. We took their road and we went on it. The white women cried, and our women laughed. But there are things which you have said to me which I do not like. They were not sweet like sugar, but bitter like gourds. You said that you wanted to put us on a reservation, to build us houses and to make us medicine lodges. I do not want them.

I was born upon the prairie, where the wind blew free, and there was nothing to break the light of the sun. I was born where there were no enclosures, and where everything drew a free breath. I want to die there, and not within walls. I know every stream and every wood between the Rio Grande and the Arkansas. I have hunted and lived over that country. I lived like my fathers before me, and like them, I lived happily.

When I was at Washington, the Great Father told me that all the Comanche land was ours, and that no one should hinder us in living upon it. So why do you ask us to leave the rivers, and the sun, and the wind, and live in houses? Do not ask us to give up the buffalo for the sheep. The young men have heard talk of this, and it has made them sad and angry. Do not speak of it more. I love to carry out the talk I get from the Great Father. When I get goods and presents, I and my people feel glad since it shows that he holds us in his eye. If the Texans had kept out of my country, there might have been peace. But that which you now say we must live on is too small.

The Texans have taken away the places where the grass grew the thickest and the timber was the best. Had we kept that, we might have done the thing you ask. But it is too late. The white man has the country which we loved and we only wish to wander on the prairie until we die. Any good thing you say to me shall not be forgotten. I shall carry it as near to my heart as my children, and it shall be as often on my tongue as the name of the Great Spirit. I want it all clear and pure, and I wish it so, that all who go through among my people may find peace when they come in, and leave it [i.e., peace] when they go out.

Ely S. Parker. Photograph, uncredited (ca. 1867). Smithsonian Institution, National Anthropological Archives.

1869

Ely S. Parker (Donehogawa, "Keeper of the Western Door of the Long House of Iroquois"), a Seneca and grandson of Red Jacket, was a brigadier general for the Union army during the Civil War. A personal friend and military secretary to General Ulysses S. Grant, he was the first Native American to be named commissioner of Indian Affairs, and in this capacity worked to improve government relations with the Indians.

In his annual report, he pointed out how the government, because of its inconsistent behavior and various duplicitous treaties, had led the Indians to believe that they were considered independent nations capable of acting for themselves, while in actuality they were treated as helpless, ignorant wards of the government. He argued for honest dealings with the Indians in the future—if they were going to be dependents, they should be treated with the protectiveness and consideration due to dependents—and for the elimination of the hypocritical attitudes that had directed government actions in the past.

> The Indian tribes of the United States are not sovereign nations, capable of making treaties, as none of them have an organized government of such inherent strength as would secure a faithful obedience of its people in the observance of compacts of this character. They are held to be wards of the government, and the only title the law concedes to them to the lands they occupy or claim is a mere possessory one. But because treaties have been made with them, generally for the extinguishment of their supposed absolute title to the land inhabited by them, or over which they roam, they have become falsely impressed with the notion of national independence. It is time that this idea should be dispelled, and the government cease the cruel farce of dealing with its helpless and ignorant wards. . . . As civilization advances and their possessions of land are required for settlement, such legislation should be granted to them as a wise, liberal, and just government ought to extend to subjects holding their dependent relation.

Chief Red Cloud (Makhpiya-luta, "Scarlet Cloud," or Makhpia-sha, "Red Cloud"), who had an impressive record as a fearless warrior, led a Sioux delegation to Washington. After visiting with President Ulysses S. Grant at the White House, he went on to New York City, where, on 14 June, he made an impassioned plea to an enthusiastic audience at Cooper Institute for the righting of wrongs that had been done to the Indians.

My brothers and my friends who are before me today, God Almighty has made us all, and He is here to hear what I have to say to you today. The Great Spirit made us both. He gave us land, and he gave you land. You came here and we received you as brothers. When the Almighty made you, he made you all white and clothed you. When he made us, He made us with red skins and poor. When you first came we were very many and you were few. You do not know who appears before you to speak. He is a representative of the original American race, the first people on this continent. We are good, and not bad. The reports which you get about us are all on one side. You hear of us only as murderers and thieves. We are not so. If we had more lands to give you, we would give them, but we have no more. We are driven into a very little island, and we want you, our dear friends, to help us with the government of the United States.

The Great Spirit made us poor and ignorant. He made you rich and wise and skillful in things which we know nothing about. The good Father made you to eat tame game, and us to eat wild game. Ask any one who has gone through to California. They will tell you we have treated them well. You have children. We, too, have children, and we wish to bring them up well. We ask you to help us do it.

At the mouth of Horse Creek [Wyoming], in 1852, the Great Father made a treaty with us. We agreed to let him pass through our territory unharmed for fifty years. We kept our word. We committed no murders, no depredations, until the troops came there. When the troops were sent there trouble and disturbance arose. Since that time there have been various goods sent from time to time to us, but only once did they reach us, and soon the Great Father took away the only good man he had sent to us, Colonel [Thomas] Fitzpatrick.* The Great Father said we must go to farming, and some of our men went to farming near Fort Laramie, and we were treated very badly indeed.

We came to Washington to see our Great Father that peace might be continued. The Great Father that made us both wishes peace to be kept; we want to keep peace. Will you help us? In 1868 men came out and brought papers. We could not read

Red Cloud. Photograph by Charles M. Bell (1880). Smithsonian Institution, National Anthropological Archives.

them, and they did not tell us what was in them. We thought the treaty was to remove the forts, and that we should then cease from fighting. But they wanted to send us traders on the Missouri. We did not want to go to the Missouri, but wanted traders where we were. When I reached Washington, the Great Father explained to me what the treaty was, and showed me that the interpreters had deceived me. All I want is right and justice. I have tried to get from the Great Father what is right and just. I have not altogether succeeded. I want you to help me get what is right and just. I represent the whole Sioux Nation, and they will be bound by what I say. I am no Spotted Tail [another Sioux leader], to say one thing one day and be bought for a pin the next. Look at me, I am poor and naked, but I am the chief of the nation. We do not want riches but we do want to train our children right. Riches would do us no good. We could not take them with us to the other world. We do not want riches. We want peace and love.

The riches that we have in this world, Secretary [of the Interior Jacob] Cox said truly, we cannot take with us to the next world. Then I wish to know why commissioners are sent out to us who do nothing but rob us and get the riches of this world away from us? I was brought up among the traders and those who came out there in the early times treated me well and I had a good time with them. They taught us to wear clothes and to use tobacco and ammunition. But by and by, the Great Father sent out a different kind of men; men who cheated and drank whiskey; men who were so bad that the Great Father could not keep them at home and so sent them out there.

I have sent a great many words to the Great Father but they never reached him. They were drowned on the way, and I was afraid the words I spoke lately to the Great Father would not reach you, so I came to speak to you myself; and now I am going away to my home. I want to have men sent out to my people whom we know and can trust. I am glad I have come here. You belong in the East, and I belong in the West, and I am glad I have come here and that we understand one another. I am very much obliged to you for listening to me. I go home this afternoon. I hope you will think of what I have said to you. I bid you all an affectionate farewell.

*The agent at the Upper Platte agency, which was about 100 miles from Fort Laramie.

Spotted Tail. Photograph by Alexander Gardner (1872). Smithsonian Institution, National Anthropological Archives.

1877

The Brulé chief Spotted Tail (Sinte-galeska) at first counseled his tribe to accept the white men's way of life. But over the years many questions arose in his mind, as he observed the whites' contradictory behavior and broken promises. His people had been approached successively and "converted" by several groups of Christians, each of which had insisted that they followed the only right way of life. One day, Spotted Tail questioned Captain G. M. Randall of the 23d U.S. Infantry, whom the Indians called "Black Beard," about the contradictions he had noted in Christianity.

I am bothered what to believe. Some years ago, a good man, as I think, came to us. He talked me out of all my old faith; and after a while, thinking that he must know more of these matters than an ignorant Indian, I joined his church and became a Methodist. After a while he went away; another man came and talked, and I became a Baptist; then another came and talked and I became a Presbyterian. Now another one has come, and wants me to be an Episcopalian. What do you think of it? . . . All these people tell different stories, and each wants me to believe that his special way is the only way to be good and save my soul. I have about made up my mind that either they all lie, or that they don't know any more about it than I did at first. I have always believed in the Great Spirit, and worshipped him in my own way. These people don't seem to want to change my belief in the Great Spirit, but to change my way of talking to him. White men have education and books, and ought to know what to do, but hardly any two of them agree on what should be done.

Crazy Horse and his band of Sioux on their way from Camp Sheridan to surrender to General George Crook. Note the horse-drawn travois used to convey children and personal belongings. Engraving from a sketch by Hottes, from Frank Leslie's Weekly, (9 June 1877). Courtesy of The New-York Historical Society, New York City.

1877

Little Hawk was with Crazy Horse when the famous Oglala Sioux chief (whom the historian John Tebbel has called "the true genius of the Sioux"), after years of intense fighting with the whites, finally surrendered to General George Crook on 6 May at the Red Cloud Agency, Nebraska. Bitterly, Little Hawk accused both soldiers and settlers of having themselves instigated the trouble that had since decimated his tribe, and condemned Crook's duplicity.

> Yes, I have been what you white men call a hostile and I am not sorry. We lived in our country in the way our fathers and fathers' fathers lived before us, and we sought trouble with no men. But the soldiers came into our country and fired upon us and we fought back. Is it so bad to fight in defense of one's country and loved ones? Remember that it was not the Indian who made war in the white man's country, but always the whites pushing in, killing our women and children, burning our homes, taking everything from us.
>
> Finally, your scouts came to us, saying that if we would stop fighting and come in to Three Stars [General George Crook], he would help us get an agency in our own country. We were tired of fighting and running from the soldiers, so we came. And now that we are here, we understand that we are to be pushed into another place, an unknown country. . . . I have only one more thing to say. Are you the same men the scouts represented to us as being the great Three Stars, the soldier-chief who speaks to all men with a straight tongue?

This pictograph by the Oglala Sioux artist Amos Bad Heart Bull shows his impression of Crazy Horse's death at Fort Robinson. Restrained by a soldier and a treacherous Indian scout, Crazy Horse is bayonetted by a second guard as they struggle in front of the guardhouse. From Amos Bad Heart Bull, A Pictographic History of the Oglala Sioux (Lincoln, University of Nebraska Press, 1967). Reprinted by courtesy of University of Nebraska Press.

1877

Following his surrender to General Crook, Crazy Horse was confined to a reservation along with other members of his tribe. He escaped in order to take his sick wife to visit her relatives at the Spotted Tail Agency, but when he got there he was arrested.

Crazy Horse agreed to return to Fort Robinson, Nebraska, on the condition that he be allowed to discuss the future of his people, who were miserable on their reservation, with the camp commandant, Colonel R. S. MacKenzie. But when he arrived at the fort, under guard, MacKenzie refused to speak with him, and he was pushed into the guard house. Outraged by this new trickery on the part of the whites, Crazy Horse tried to escape, but was mortally wounded by a guard who thrust a bayonet into his back.

Before he died on 5 September, Crazy Horse once more denounced the whites, addressing himself to Captain Lee, the military agent at the Spotted Tail Agency, who had brought him to Fort Robinson.

I was not hostile to the white man. Occasionally my young men would attack a party of the Crows or Arickarees, and take care of their ponies, but just as often, they were the assailants. We had buffalo for food and their hides for clothing, and we preferred the chase to a life of idleness and the bickerings and jealousies, as well as the frequent periods of starvation at the agencies.

But the Gray Fox (General Crook) came out in the snow and bitter cold, and destroyed my village. All of us would have perished of exposure and hunger had we not recaptured our ponies.

Then Long Hair (General Custer) came in the same way. They say we massacred him, but he would have massacred us had we not defended ourselves and fought to the death. Our first impulse was to escape with our squaws and papooses, but we were so hemmed in that we had to fight. . . .

Again the Gray Fox sent soldiers to surround me and my village; but I was tired of fighting. All I wanted was to be let alone, so I anticipated their coming, and marched all night to Spotted Tail Agency while the troops were approaching the site of my camp. Touch-the-Clouds [Crazy Horse's friend at the Spotted Tail Agency] knows how I settled at Spotted Tail Agency, in peace. The agent told me I must first talk with the big white chief of the Black Hills. Under his care I came here unarmed, but instead of talking, they tried to confine me, and when I made an effort to escape, a soldier ran his bayonet into me.

I have spoken.

1879

On 14 January, Chief Joseph (Hinmaton Yalatkit, "Thunder Rolling in the Heights"), a famous orator of the Nez Percé tribe, spoke eloquently to a large group of diplomats, cabinet members, congressmen, and other important bureaucrats in Washington, D.C. He detailed the history of Nez Percé– white relations, deplored the many inequities his people had suffered at the hands of the whites, and criticized government duplicity in a manner that foreshadowed the outspoken accusations of militant Indians of the 20th century.

I have shaken hands with a great many friends, but there are some things I want to know which no one seems able to explain. I cannot understand how the Government sends out a man to fight us, as it did General [Nelson A.] Miles, and then breaks his word. [General Miles had promised that if Joseph surrendered, his people would be returned to their own part of the country; instead they had been sent to Fort Leavenworth, Kansas.] Such a government has something wrong about it. I cannot understand

142

Chief Joseph. Photograph by Edward S. Curtis. Smithsonian Institution, National Anthropological Archives.

why so many chiefs are allowed to talk so many different ways, and promise so many different things. I have seen the Great Father Chief [President Rutherford B. Hayes], the next Great Chief [Secretary of the Interior Carl Schurz], the Commissioner chief [Commissioner of Indian Affairs Ezra A. Hayt], the Law chief [General Benjamin Franklin Butler], and many other law chiefs [congressmen], and they all say they are my friends, and that I shall have justice, but while their mouths all talk right I do not understand why nothing is done for my people. I have heard talk and talk, but nothing is done. Good words do not last long unless they amount to something. Words do not pay for my dead people. They do not pay for my country, now overrun by white men. They do not protect my father's grave. They do not pay for all my horses and cattle. Good words will not give me back my children. Good words will not make good the promise of your War chief General Miles. Good words will not give my people good health and stop them from dying. Good words will not get my people a home where they can live in peace and take care of themselves. I am tired of talk that comes to nothing. It makes my heart sick when I remember all the good words and all the broken promises. There has been too much talking by men who had no right to talk. Too many misrepresentations have been made, too many misunderstandings have come up between the white men about the Indians. If the white man wants to live in peace with the Indian he can live in peace. There need be no trouble. Treat all men alike. Give them the same law. Give them an even chance to live and grow. All men were made by the same Great Spirit Chief. They are all brothers. The earth is the mother of all people, and all people should have equal rights upon it. You might as well expect the rivers to run backward as that any man who was born a free man should be contented when penned up and denied liberty to go where he pleases. If you tie a horse to a stake, do you expect he will grow fat? If you pen an Indian up on a small spot of earth, and compel him to stay there, he will not be contented, nor will he grow and prosper. I have asked some of the great white chiefs where they get their authority to say to the Indian that he shall stay in one place, while he sees white men going where they please. They cannot tell me.

I only ask of the government to be treated as all other men are treated. If I cannot go to my own home, let me have a home in some country where my people will not die so fast. . . .

When I think of our condition my heart is heavy. I see men of my race treated as outlaws and driven from country to country or shot down like animals.

I know that my race must change. We cannot hold our own

with white men as we are. We ask only an even chance to live as other men live. We ask to be recognized as men. We ask that the same law shall work alike on all men. If the Indian breaks the law, punish him by the law. If the white man breaks the law, punish him also.

Let me be a free man—free to travel, free to stop, free to work, free to trade where I choose, free to choose my own teachers, free to follow the religion of my fathers, free to think and talk and act for myself—and I will obey every law, or submit to the penalty.

Whenever the white man treats an Indian as they treat each other, then we will have no more wars. We shall all be alike—brothers of one father and one mother, with one mother, with one sky above us and one country around us, and one government for all. Then the Great Spirit Chief who rules above will smile upon this land, and send rain to wash out the bloody spots made by brothers' hands from the face of the earth. For this time the Indian race are waiting and praying. I hope that no more groans of wounded men and women will ever go to the ear of the Great Spirit Chief above, and that all people may be one people.

In-mut-too-yah-lat-lat [Chief Joseph] has spoken for his people.

The council meeting between General George Crook and Geronimo and his band of Apaches in Mexico, March 1886. Geronimo is seated third from the left in the front row; General Crook is second from the right. Photograph by C. S. Fly in Martin F. Schmitt and Dee Brown, Fighting Indians of the West (New York, 1948). Smithsonian Institution, National Anthropological Archives.

1886

Geronimo (Goyathlay, "The Yawner," "One Who Yawns"), a Chiricahua Apache war chief, and one of the most famous Indians of the 19th century, was feared by both the Americans and the Mexicans. When the Americans tried to move his tribe from Apache Pass, Arizona, to San Carlos, another Indian reservation in the territory already housing seven Apache bands, Geronimo and a large body of followers who did not want to be confined on yet another reservation fled into Mexico. There they raided Mexican livestock and sold them to American traders. Brought back to San Carlos by the army, Geronimo and seventy Chiricahua warriors then escaped to the Sierra Madre range in Mexico. After six months of raiding there, they returned to San Carlos and freed all the remaining Apaches who wanted to escape from the reservation and domination by the U.S. Army which controlled it. Once again in Mexico, the band were cornered by a Mexican regiment, and most of the men and women who had gone with them were killed, but Geronimo remained free. In 1883, the United States government sent a detachment under General George Crook to deal with the Chiricahuas. While Geronimo was off raiding, Crook captured his base camp, together with all the remaining women and children. At that point, in order to avoid further conflict, Geronimo tried to make peace with Crook, and to settle down to an agricultural life. In February 1884 he and his subchiefs rejoined those Apaches left on the reservation and began to develop profitable ranches.

The press, ignoring the boredom, unhappiness, and restrictive conditions that had made the Apaches run in the first place, presented a distorted picture of the Indians and their actions. Geronimo was depicted as a villain, and Crook as his victim—it was reported, erroneously, that he had surrendered to Geronimo. In May 1885, distressed by the newspaper accounts and tired of a life to which he was not suited, Geronimo—and 134 warriors—left for new raids. Crook again pursued the chief, and in May

1886 caught up with the band. He warned them that future attempts to escape would result in exile to Florida. Finally convinced that he should surrender and return to the reservation, Geronimo told General Crook that much of his reputation as a troublemaker had stemmed from the reprehensible actions of the whites (Indian agents, interpreters, and newspapermen) and the lies they had spread about him.

I was living quietly and contented, doing and thinking of no harm . . . when people began to speak bad of me. . . . I hadn't killed a horse or man, American or Indian . . . yet they said I was a bad man, and the worst man there; but what harm had I done? I did not leave on my own accord. . . . I would like to know now who it was that gave the order to arrest and hang me. I don't know what the reason was that people should speak badly of me. . . . The fault was not mine. . . .

I have several times asked for peace, but trouble has come from the agents and interpreters. . . . From this [time] on I hope that people will tell me nothing but the truth. . . . I do not want you to believe any bad papers about me. I want the papers sent you to tell the truth about me, because I want to do what is right. Very often there are stories put in the newspapers that I am to be hanged. I don't want that any more. When a man tries to do right, such stories ought not to be put in the newspapers. . . . There are very few of us left. . . . I don't want that we should be killing each other. . . .

From here on I want to live in peace. Don't believe any bad talk you hear about me. The agents and the interpreters hear that somebody has done wrong, and they blame it all on me. . . . I don't want those men who talked this way about me to be my agents any more. I want good men to be my agents and interpreters; people who will talk right. I want this peace to be legal and good. Whenever I meet you I talk good to you, and you to me, and peace is soon established; but when you go to the reservation you put agents and interpreters over us who do bad things. Perhaps they don't mind what you tell them, because I do not believe you would tell them to do bad things to us. In the future we don't want these bad men to be allowed near where we are to live. . . . I think I am a good man, but in the papers all over the world they say I am a bad man; but it is a bad thing to say about me. I never do wrong without a cause. . . .

To prove to you that I am telling you the truth, remember I sent you word that I would come from a place far away to speak to you here, and you see us now. . . . If I were thinking bad, or if I had done bad I would never have come here. If it had been my fault, would I have come so far to talk to you?

1889

Sitting Bull (Tatanko Iotake), having fought unremittingly with white men for over a decade, was no respecter of treaties signed by them. He was a staunch supporter of the Ghost Dance religion and its proscription of white customs. At a meeting of the "Silent Eaters" society of the Hunkpapa Sioux, Sitting Bull denounced the government's Indian commissioners, who negotiated for the purchase of Indian land, and accused them of betraying promises and misleading the Indians.

Friends and Relatives. Our minds are again disturbed by the Great Father's representatives, the Indian agents, the squaw-men, the mixed bloods, the interpreters, and the favorite ration chiefs. * What is it they want of us at this time? They want us to give up another chunk of our tribal land. This is not the first time or the last time. They will try to gain possession of the last piece of ground we possess. They are again telling us what they intend to do if we agree to their wishes. Have we ever set a price on our land and received such a value? No, we never did. What we got under the former treaties were promises of all sorts. They promised how we are going to live peaceably on the land we still own and how they are going to show us the new ways of living— even told us how we can go to heaven when we die, but all that we realized out of the agreements with the Great Father was, we are dying off. . . .

. . . something tells me that the Great Father's representatives have again brought with them a well-worded paper, containing just what they want but ignoring our wishes in the matter. It is this that they are attempting to drive us to. Our people are blindly deceived. Some are in favor of the proposition, but we who realize that our children and grandchildren may live a little longer, must necessarily look ahead and flatly reject the proposi-tion. I, for one, am bitterly opposed to it. The Great Father has proven himself an *unkomti* [trickster] in our past dealings.

When the white people invaded our Black Hills country [in South Dakota] our treaty agreements were still in force but the Great Father ignored it, pretending to keep out the intruders through military force, and at last, failing to keep them out, they had to let them come in and take possession of our best part of our tribal possession. Yet the Great Father maintains a very large standing army that can stop anything.

Therefore I do not wish to consider any proposition to cede any portion of our tribal holding to the Great Father. If I agree to dispose of any part of our land to the white people I would feel guilty of taking food away from our children's mouths, and I do not wish to be that mean. There are things they tell us [that]

The capture and death of Sitting Bull, who was pursued by the government for promoting the Ghost Dance and fomenting rebellion. Reproduced from the Collections of the Library of Congress.

sound good to hear, but when they have accomplished their purpose they will go home and will not try to fulfill our agreements with them.

*The men responsible for distributing the rations sent to the Indians by the government.

5
The 20th Century
"Each remaining acre is a promise . . ."

No concerted attempt had ever been made in the United States to understand the Indian point of view. By the end of the 19th century, federal government policies were again shifting, this time away from attempts to exterminate and toward enforced assimilation of a kind that had been practiced off and on for a century. The bureaucrats believed that, since the Indians appeared to be "vanishing," the process would be accelerated by destroying Indian culture and values, breaking up tribal lands, and imposing a new way of life upon the Indians. By 1897, when President William McKinley declared that Indian tribes should be dissolved, it was becoming almost impossible to enforce the treaties Indians had made with the United States. Although the Fourteenth Amendment (1868) technically made the Indians citizens of the United States, their rights were not guaranteed by statute until 1924, when full citizenship was conferred upon them officially. This was partially a way of recognizing the services of the thousands of Indians who had served in the armed forces during World War I. Indians who lived on reservations were exempted from paying taxes, and were provided with certain social services, but in many other ways continued to have marked social and economic disadvantages.

Beginning with the arrival of Mohawks from the United States during the Revolutionary War, Canada, too, had established *réserves* (reservations) for the Indians within its borders, and Indian activities were closely regulated. Métis (children of mixed Indian-white marriages) were denied privileges accorded to the full-blooded Indians; they were relegated to second-class status. In Canada, too, both the Canadian Indians and the Métis began to demand full citizenship. The Métis rose up against the government of Canada in abortive attempts to establish an independent state within its borders, but their attempts led to failure and the eventual execution of their leader, Louis Riel, who was hanged for treason in 1885.

Most 20th-century Canadian Indians have rejected assimilation, favoring instead a form of self-rule that features Indian-elected councils, which in turn govern the individual *réserves*. These Indians can now conduct their own business with the outside world, but the ownership of their homelands continues to reside in the crown and in the government of Canada itself. Métis' protests have carried forward the spirit of Louis Riel, but their status has hardly improved since his era. The Canadian Indians have continued to fight the notion that the government of Canada has the right to dispose of their lands to outside interests, a struggle once more made public when the Crees took the Canadian government to court in 1972 in a partially successful attempt to prevent the takeover of some of their best hunting and fishing lands for the construction of the James Bay Hydroelectric Project. The Indians, in this case, won a settlement of $100 million, 25% in royalties, and the guarantee to them of certain valuable lands in perpetuity.

The Eskimos, although culturally distinct from the American Indians, have been found by anthropologists to be to some extent racially linked to them. Both groups came across the Bering Strait from Siberia. The American Indians spread out over the continents of North and South America; the Eskimos remained in the circumpolar region. At the present time, the North American Eskimos, also known as Inuits, live in northern Canada, Greenland, and Alaska. Their nomadic life and lack of tribal or national links have until recently isolated them from most of the outside world, even though they have participated actively in the economic development of the areas where they live.

In the past twenty years, heightened efforts to industrialize areas in which the Eskimos live and to develop natural resources such as the oil and natural gas found in Prudhoe Bay, Alaska, and the Beaufort Sea, Canada, have begun to pose threats to their survival. Although in some instances compensation has been made for the millions of acres now being worked by whites, this does not change the fact that the natural bases of Eskimo culture, life style, and basic physical survival have been threatened. Living in urban environments, as many of them have been forced to do by creeping industrialization, has weakened them physically, and their family life has been disrupted by this and by an educational system that necessitates attendance at boarding school once students are past the early grades.

In 1982 the Inuit Circumpolar Conference, a militant civil rights organization embracing groups from all three areas inhabited by them, was organized. Headed by Hans-Pavia Rosing, a Greenland Eskimo, these disparate groups have joined in the common cause of protecting their environment and traditional culture from further unauthorized incursions by white men. They make forceful protests against the disruption of the ecological balance in the Arctic, and have achieved recognition for the Eskimos as a viable, independent political and economic entity. According to James Stott, an Eskimo from Barrow, Alaska, who is a member of the Conference, it was the potentially destructive conflict between Western and Eskimo culture that acted as the catalyst for their unification and militant actions.

The Indians of the Caribbean have lost their ethnic identity and are no longer recognizable as separate tribal or racial groups. In Central and South America the situation varies widely from one country to another. Indian languages and cultures persist more strongly in those countries that still have large surviving indigenous populations, although Indians have been to a certain extent absorbed into the total population through intermarriage with whites. Perhaps the most destructive situation has been that in Brazil. There the first settlers had destroyed Indian villages, captured and enslaved the survivors on the plantations of Maranhão and Pará. Others, as we have seen, were converted to Christianity and were forced to work on Jesuit reservations. In some ways Brazilian Indians have never recovered from the original depredations, and in the 20th century some tribes, still facing the threat of genocide, are withdrawing deeper into the Mato Grosso.

In 1910 Marshal Cândido Mariano da Silva Rondón, himself reputed to be of Indian ancestry, founded the Serviço de Proteção aos Indios (SPI). In a distinct departure from traditional Brazilian attitudes toward Indian participation in the life of Brazil, the goal of SPI was to develop greater interaction—social and educational—between the Indians and other Brazilians. Rondón never lived to see his dream realized, and it may even have been a dangerous one, since it resulted in bringing the Indians out of the jungles and into the open, where they were more vulnerable to hostile forces. Although in the 1960s anthropologists Claudio and Orlando Villas Boas succeeded in securing the creation of Xingu National Park, a protected area, the numbers of Brazilian Indians are still diminishing, and charges of genocide—of deliberate attempts to exterminate the Indians—have been leveled against the Brazilian government by interest groups and the press.

Like their North American counterparts, South American tribes now openly condemn white efforts to recreate the Indians in their own—white—image. Taken to São Paulo by a white man for medical treatment in 1971, Tawapuh, a Wausha tribesman, was highly critical of urban life, calling the air foul, the food unpalatable, the sexual mores ridiculous, and the constant presence of the military police incomprehensible among people belonging to the same society. Furthermore, he was amazed that any white man, after having sampled the beauty and freedom of Wausha tribal life, would want to return to the city.

Throughout the Americas, a desire to maintain the distinctive culture of individual tribes has been replaced by a sense of multi-tribal nationalism (Pan-Indianism). This is characterized by an interest in traditional religion on the part of young Indians, with religious observance often accompanied by political awareness and activism. Native Americans are speaking out for themselves and firmly demanding their rights as citizens and as the original inhabitants of the Americas. Aware of their heritage, they are no longer content to be treated as second-class citizens, and want to be masters of their own destiny. The Indians who speak out now are able to do so in fluent English, are less vulnerable to discreditation than their ancestors, and many hold positions of importance. They have won recognition from whites in many fields—literature, the arts, education, the armed forces, politics—and frequently have used their abilities and influence to ameliorate social conditions among their own people. They continue to work for the return of the lands that they insist have been wrongfully taken from them, and for the self-government and self-determination that they believe is rightfully theirs.

Today's Indians have a bicultural perspective. They know what they want to preserve from their own traditional culture, and what they want to acquire from white culture, as well as what they find unacceptable about that culture. Their message is forceful and clear, and demonstrates their continuing adherence to the basic values of their ancestors and their enduring reverence for the land.

They are no longer content to operate with tribal, or even regional, frameworks. The concept of Red Power, promoted by Pan-Indian movements such as the Association on American Indian Affairs (AAIA), the National Congress of American Indians (NCAI), the American Indian Movement (AIM), the American Indian Historical Society, and others, has challenged in court the old denigrating stereotypes and demanded through legal channels the correction of wrongs done to American Indians in the past. The Native American Rights Fund has fought a number of major cases involving Indian land and water rights. Activist groups such as the National Indian Youth Council (NIYC) have staged public demonstrations to dramatize and demand redress for past wrongs. These include the Kinzua Dam protests (1960), the Washington State fish-ins (1968), the seizing of Alcatraz Island (1969), the takeover of the Bureau of Indian Affairs (BIA) building in Washington, D.C. (1972), and many other actions geared to forcing the government to restore what the Indians feel is rightfully theirs.

Such Indian activists as Clyde Warrior (Ponca), Melvin Thom (Nevada Paiute), Robert Blatchford (Navajo), and Bruce Wilkie (Makah) forcefully rejected white patronage and dependence of the Indians on the white men. From them the movement for Red Power and self-determination received its first impetus. In 1961, at the American Indian Chicago Conference, Indians formulated their plan for their future in America. Russell Means (Oglala Sioux), Vine Deloria, Jr. (Standing Rock Sioux), and many others have also led campaigns to restore to the North American Indians the lands they consider to have been stolen from them. And in 1970, the Zuñi became the first tribe to run their own political and economic affairs through a formal council. In July of that same year, President Nixon spoke out in favor of Indian "self-determination without termination" (of the reservations). The Indians, he said, should be respected as individuals, and should be given aid to help them overcome problems caused by poverty, poor health, inadequate education, and substandard housing. In other words, they must be able to remain Indians while they exercise their rights as Americans, and they are no longer to be subjected to stifling paternalism. This led to historic changes in government policy toward the Indians, recognition of the idea of self-government allowing other Indian tribes to adopt the Zuñi plan in whole or in part.

In 1977, more than sixty tribes of North, Central, and South America attended an international non-governmental organization (NGO) conference which had as its theme "Discrimination Against Indigenous Populations in the Americas." Held in Geneva, Switzerland, it included such well-known Indian spokesmen as Vine Deloria, Jr., Ed Burnstick of the Canadian Cree, Antonio Millape, who represented 900,000 Mapuche Indians of Chile, and José Mendoza Acosta, who spoke for an organization called the Indigenous People of Panama. All demanded international consideration of their rights as sovereign nations.

The following year, ten major Indian and Native (a term which may refer to both Indians and Eskimos) organizations met in Canada, among them the Canadian Native Indian Brotherhood, the Navajo Nation, and the Alaskan Natives, and resulted in the formation of the International Indian Treaty Council, which has now become the international body representing the entire North American Indian group. Affiliated with the United Nations, the Council provides that organization with data on Indian mining rights, treaties, and the activities of organizations like the Native American Rights Fund. In the opinion of the Council, the Indian tribes *do* constitute a single sovereign nation (in keeping with the spirit of Pan-Indianism), and should therefore have the right of self-determination.

Simple survival is no longer the major issue facing most Indians. Rather, it is the quality of their future as self-sufficient human beings that may be jeopardized by current conditions. Having already survived five centuries of repression, the Indians—whether they live on reservations or not—are eager to free themselves from the shackles of the past so that they can once more live a life of their own choosing.

1915

Dr. Carlos Montezuma (Wassaja, "Signaling," "Becoming") born an Apache, was captured by Pima Indians when he was six years old and sold to a traveling photographer for $30. His mother was refused permission to leave their reservation to look for him, and was later killed by an Indian scout after she defied the local Indian agent's orders and left anyway. Montezuma held the reservation system, and the Bureau of Indian Affairs (BIA) which controlled it, responsible for his mother's death, and never forgave it for that and for denying the Indians control of their own actions.

154

(a) Dr. Carlos Montezuma. Photograph, (ca. 1915). Reproduced from the Arizona Historical Society Library.

Montezuma graduated with honors from the University of Illinois, and received his M.D. from the Chicago Medical School. He gave up private practice to become active in Indian affairs and, feeling that the BIA had a stranglehold on Indian life and that it prevented the development of Indian autonomy, was a vocal opponent of the Bureau and its methods of operation. From his own funds he founded and subsidized *Wassaja*, a militant Indian journal taking his own name, which was outspoken in its distrust of the government, and called for the unity of all Indian tribes, cutting across individual tribal ties.

Speaking at the Conference of the Society of American Indians in Lawrence, Kansas, on 30 September, he berated those Indians who had accepted jobs in the BIA, and called for its abolition as an absolute necessity if the Indians were to become productive human beings in modern society, on their own terms.

> Indian employees of the Indian Service are working against the freedom of their race. . . .
>
> The Indian Bureau is the only obstacle that stands in the way, that hinders our people's freedom. . . . We Indians must fight and kill the very organ that was organized to free us in order to free ourselves. . . .
>
> It is appalling and inexplicable that the palefaces have taken all of the Indian's property—the continent of America—which was all he had in the world. . . . The Indian asks for public school, college, and university education for his children. . . . Will the department defray the expenses of any college or university Indian students? . . .
>
> To dominate a race you do not want to educate them. . . .
>
> The life of the Indian Bureau is supported by plausibilities and

(b) *The logo of Dr. Montezuma's paper* Wassaja, *shown here, forcefully depicts his belief that the Bureau of Indian Affairs acted as a potent deterrent to Indian enterprise, and that the only salvation for the Indians lay in freeing themselves from the shackles imposed by white bureaucracy. From Arnold Marquis,* A Guide to America's Indians: Ceremonials, Reservations, and Museums *(Norman, Okla., 1974). © 1974 by the University of Oklahoma Press.*

by civil service. . . .

The Indian Bureau system is wrong. The only way to adjust wrong is to abolish it, and the only reform is to let my people go. After freeing the Indian from the shackles of government supervision, what is the Indian going to do: Leave that with the Indian, and it is none of your business.

The iron band of the Indian Bureau has us in charge. The slimy clutches of horrid greed and selfish interests are gripping the Indian's property. Little by little the Indian's land and everything else is fading into a dim and unknown realm.

The Indian's prognosis is bad—unfavorable, no hope . . . when all the Indian's money in the United States Treasury is disposed of; when the Indian's property is all taken from him; when the Indians have nothing in this wide, wide world; when the Indians will have no rights, no place to lay their heads; and when the Indians will be permitted to exist only on the outskirts of the towns; when they must go to the garbage boxes in alleys to keep them[selves] from starving; when the Indians will be driven into the streets, and finally the streets will be no place for them, what will the Indian Bureau do for them? Nothing, but drop them. The Indian Bureau will go out of business. . . .

The abolishment of the Indian Bureau will not only benefit the Indians, but the country will derive more money annually from the Indians than the government has appropriated to them. . . . by doing away with the Indian Bureau you stop making paupers and useless beings and start the making of producers and workers.

Plenty Coups. Photograph by C. M. Bell (1880). Smithsonian Institution, National Anthropological Archives.

1928

Plenty Coups (Aleekchea'ahoosh, "Many Achievements"), a Crow war chief, had a prophetic dream that the whites would eventually conquer the country, and therefore urged his men to join with the whites to fight against the Sioux. He won renown as a scout with the U.S. Army and fought with General George Crook against the "hostiles" (Indians who refused to surrender to the U.S. government), led by Crazy Horse. When the last of the great buffalo herds was destroyed in the 1880s, he urged the Indians to adjust to the demands of the white men, and saw education as the only means by which Indians could escape from poverty and from victimization.

In 1928 he decided to deed his two hundred acres of beautiful valley land near Pryor Canyon (Montana), as "a monument to the friendship I have always felt for the white people."

A large group of Indians and white men gathered before his cabin to commemorate this occasion, and Brigadier General James G. Harboard, representing the Department of the Interior, accepted the gift of land for use in perpetuity as a public park and camping ground for all people, irrespective of race. Speaking through interpreter John Frost, himself a Crow Indian, the eighty-year old chief dwelt on his friendship with the whites and pleaded with them for fair treatment of the Indians.

Many snows have fallen, marking the years I have lived at peace with my white neighbors. No red man has ever been shown so many honors as have I.

My people—the Crow Nation—have not always been treated fairly. They hold no hate.

Today I, who have been called the Chief of Chiefs among red men, present to all the children of our Great White Father this land where snows for more than fifty years have fallen on my tipi.

This park is not to be a memorial to me, but to the Crow Nation. It is given as a token of my friendship for all people, both red and white.

The Great Spirit is good to all His children, but it seems He loves His white children most. He has never shown my people how to do the many wonderful things His white children are doing. He did give us patience and love of home and children.

Our old men have long pondered this matter in their councils, and we have now come to believe it is because we were late in finding the true God.

Today one of our noblest red men [Vice-President Curtis] has been chosen to represent this nation as a subchief to the Great White Father. As the coming ages pass, you will hear of many others of my race holding places of high honor and trust.

My people have ever been fighting men, and I believe the warrior ranks highest among all professional men. He fights for his women, his children, and his home. Therefore, Chief War Eagle [the Crow name selected for General Harboard], my heart goes out to you because you, too, are a great warrior who has done great service for our country. On behalf of my people, I invite you into the Crow tribe—the highest honor within my power.

And as the snows of coming winters go by, I hope you will keep in mind the needs of my people in their struggle to be better Americans.

May the Great Spirit permit your moccasins to make tracks in many snows is my prayer. I have spoken.

This early photograph of Will Rogers, ca. 1905, shows him in the cowboy costume he wore in his stage performances. Courtesy of the Will Rogers Memorial Commission.

1930s

Will Rogers, one of the most famous humorists of the 20th century, was part Cherokee. He was a performer on stage, screen, and radio, as well as a speaker and writer. His keen analyses of world events won him respect and affection throughout the world, and they remain valid today. Here is an example of his ironic recounting of Cherokee history as it appeared in a newspaper column syndicated throughout the United States:

159

Old Andy [Andrew Jackson] . . . is the one that run us Cherokees out of Georgia and North Carolina. . . . Old Andy, every time he couldn't find any one to jump on, would come back and pounce onto us Indians. Course he licked the English down in New Orleans, but he didn't do it till the war had been over two weeks, so he just really fought them as an encore. Then he would go to Florida and shoot up the Seminoles. . . . Then he would have a row with the government, and they would take his command and his liquor away from him, and he would come back and sick himself onto us Cherokees again. . . .

Old Andy made the White House. . . . The Indians wanted him in there so he would let us alone for awhile. Andy stayed two terms. . . . He had to get back to his regular business, which was shooting at the Indians. They were for a third term for Andy. They sent the Indians to Oklahoma. They had a treaty that said, "You shall have this land as long as grass grows and water flows." It was not only a good rhyme but looked like a good treaty, and it was till they struck oil. Then the government took it away from us again. They said the treaty only refers to "water and grass; it don't say anything about oil."

So the Indians lost another bet. The first one was to Andrew Jackson, and the second was to Rockefeller, Doheny, Sinclair, and Socony. . . .

It was our tribe of Cherokees that sold the original Cherokee Strip. . . .

I think the government only give us about a dollar an acre for it. We had it for hunting grounds, but we never knew enough to hunt oil on it. I can remember as a kid the payment we had, when the government paid out the money to the Cherokees for it. There was something over three million dollars as there was that many acres and we got about $320 apiece, I think it was.

The Cherokees are supposed to be the highest civilized tribe there is and yet that's all we ever got in all our lifetime and sold a fortune in oil and wonderful agricultural land to get that little $320 apiece. Yet there was the Osages lived right by us and they get that much before breakfast every morning, and they are supposed to be uncivilized.

So it really shows you it kinder pays not to know too much. I would trade my so-called superior knowledge right now for an Osage headright. If you had their payments you wouldn't need to know anything only where the payment was going to be held. But as a matter of fact the Osages got some mighty smart men among them.

Luther Standing Bear. Smithsonian Institution, National Anthropological Archives.

1933

Chief Luther Standing Bear, an Oglala Sioux, spent many years away from his reservation, first as a student at Carlisle, and then in a variety of occupations. For two years, he performed with Buffalo Bill's Wild West Show, and he later became an actor and consultant in Hollywood for movies about the Indians. When he returned to the reservation in 1931, after a sixteen-year absence, he was horrified by the conditions under which his people were living. Two years later, in response to what he had seen, he published the second of his four books, *Land of the Spotted Eagle*, in which he was outspoken in his criticism of federal Indian policy, and of the attitudes of government bureaucracy toward the Indians.

The Indian is a natural conservationist. . . .

There was a great difference in the attitude taken by the Indian and the Caucasian toward nature, and this difference made of one a conservationist and of the other a nonconservationist of life. . . . The philosophy of the Caucasian was, "Things of the

161

earth, earthy"—to be belittled and despised. Bestowing upon himself the position and title of a superior creature, others in the scheme were, in the natural order of things, of inferior position and title; and this attitude dominated his actions toward all things. The worth and right to live were his, thus he heartlessly destroyed. . . .

The feathered and blanketed figure of the American Indian has come to symbolize the American continent. . . .

The white man does not understand the Indian for the reason that he does not understand America. He is too far removed from its formative processes. . . . The man from Europe is still a foreigner and an alien. And he still hates the man who questioned his path across the continent.

The attempted transformation of the Indian by the white man and the chaos that has resulted are but the fruits of the white man's disobedience of a fundamental and spiritual law.

The pressure that has been brought to bear upon the native people, since the cessation of armed conflict, in the attempt to force conformity of custom and habit, has caused a reaction more destructive than war, and the injury has not only affected the Indian, but has extended to the white population as well. Tyranny, stupidity, and lack of vision have brought about the situation now alluded to as the "Indian Problem."

There is, I insist, no Indian problem as created by the Indian himself. Every problem that exists today in regard to the native population is due to the white man's cast of mind. . . .

True, the white man brought great change. But the varied fruits of his civilization, though highly colored and inviting, are sickening and deadening. And if it be the part of civilization to maim, rob, and thwart, then what is progress? . . .

Regarding the "civilization" that has been thrust upon me since the days of reservation, it has not added one whit to my sense of justice; to my reverence for the rights of life; to my love for truth, honesty, and generosity; nor to my faith in Wakan Tanka—God of the Lakotas. For after all the great religions have been preached and expounded, or have been revealed by brilliant scholars, or have been written in fine books and embellished in fine language with finer covers, man—all man—is still confronted with the Great Mystery.

So if today I had a young mind to direct, to start on the journey of life, and I was faced with the duty of choosing between the natural way of my forefathers and that of the white man's present way of civilization, I would, for its welfare, unhesitatingly set that child's foot in the path of my forefathers. I would raise him to be an Indian!

Chief Kadashan's house in Wrangell, Alaska, is an excellent example of some of the effects of white influence in the area. The multi-story house is built in the European style, with vertical instead of horizontal planks. Yet the traditional totem poles stand proudly on either side of the doorway. But Indians' adoption of white ways has done little to relieve continuing social and economic pressures—and the resultant shame and alcoholism—deplored by Ruth Muskrat Bronson. Smithsonian Institution, National Anthropological Archives.

1947

Speaking at the annual meeting of the Indian Rights Association in January, Ruth Muskrat Bronson, a Cherokee, bitterly castigated the United States government for its mistreatment of the Indians of southeastern Alaska. She compared their situation to that of the Indians in the 19th century. She demonstrated how, in spite of the fact that the Tlingits and the Haidas shared certain cultural standards and patterns of behavior with the whites (i.e., a desire for the accumulation of personal wealth, competitiveness, and the practice of extensive trading), and had been able to adapt to the political and economic pressures of modern life more easily in consequence, they were nevertheless discriminated against because of their race. She pleaded for an investigation of abuses, for watchdog action on the part of Indian organizations to protect Indian property and personal rights, and for legal help to insure the passage of legislation favorable to the Alaskan Indians.

The Indians know they are . . . fighting a situation which they see clearly has a single, inevitable ending if help does not come to them soon. . . . a propertyless, marginal existence on the fringes of dependency so long as they survive as a race. . . . They are being stripped of their property by every means possible, sometimes even by agencies of our Government which has sworn to protect them. . . . They are being pushed ruthlessly and inexorably lower and lower in the economic scale, not because they are less able but because they are defenseless under discriminatory laws and practices. . . .

These passionately proud people who were once top men in this region cannot endure the constant and grueling slights put upon them. Alcohol to the point of oblivion offers one sure means of respite. . . .

Not enough land resources are now in actual possession of these Indians to guarantee a decent standard of living on a civilized basis. . . .

Here is a fight before us that is immediate and urgent. . . . We cannot ignore our responsibility.

Indian woman at the San Ildefonso pueblo in New Mexico, baking bread in a large outdoor oven. The use of these ovens is one of the traditions threatened by the advance of white civilization, and defended by Daisy Albert. Courtesy of the New Mexico Commerce & Industry Department, Tourism & Travel Division.

1954

At an intertribal symposium in Arizona, representatives of the Apache, Cherokee, and Hopi tribes discussed the ways in which the coming of the white men, and the imposition of modern civilization, had affected them. Some of the speeches made by participants were reproduced verbatim in the August issue of *The Rotarian*. Daisy Albert, a housewife from the local Hopi village of Moencopi, took a strong stand in her evaluation of the negative effects of the white men's actions toward the Indians, and warned against new dangers.

> In the old days our ancestors fought for land which was their own, and for their way of living. But the white man took our morale away from us by trying to "civilize" us. He has trampled on the Indians since he set foot in America and has destroyed everything which is good in the Indian culture, or tried to. He worked his way into the Indians' confidence with bribes, lies, and promises. . . .
>
> The white man has forced himself upon the Indian nation of America to be their "guardian." He has tried to take everything the Indians had, talking his way with sweet language and promises. These promises have not yet been fulfilled.
>
> New laws are being promoted in Congress, laws which would sever our tribal relations. They would bring in hordes of people alien to our ways. These are laws aimed at obliterating us.

All that remains of the Cornplanter grant today is this neglected monument. Photograph, record group no. 12, courtesy of the Department of Highways, Pennsylvania Historical and Museum Commission.

1960

The Seneca Indians of the Allegany Reservation strongly opposed the construction of the Kinzua Dam and Reservoir in Pennsylvania, since the project would flood land that had been given to them under the Treaty of 1794—a third of the reservation, site of the Cornplanter monument, including land the Senecas considered sacred. The Indians voted to bar U.S. Army engineers who wanted to survey the area. Despite this, they were unable to block construction of the dam, but were later able, with the help of Quakers, to receive damages of $15,000,573 for the lands and homes which had been destroyed.

In an early stage of the Indians' protest, George D. Heron, president of the Seneca Nation, testified to the House Subcommittee on Indian Affairs about what he felt were the tribe's rights.

> I live on the Allegany Reservation in New York. . . . my friends from Pennsylvania have said that the Treaty of 11 November 1794 was abrogated when all Indians became citizens in 1924. I would like to point out that the 1794 Treaty was signed by the *Seneca Nation,* not by individual Seneca Indians, and the Nation has not yet become a citizen. It remains today exactly what it was 165 years ago—in the words of the courts as reported to us by our attorney, Mr. [Arthur] Lazarus, a "quasi-sovereign independent nation." More important, our tribal lawyer tells me that the Supreme Court of the United States has held not once, but at least a dozen times, that the grant of citizenship does not affect any Indian treaty rights or in any other way change the special relationship of Indians and their property to the Federal government. I am not an educated man, but it seems very strange to me that these lawyers from Pennsylvania are willing to say that the Supreme Court ruled against the Senecas, when it did not even hear the case, while at the same time they are ignoring a whole series of actual Supreme Court decisions which go against their arguments.

I am proud to be an American citizen, and have four years in the United States Navy to prove it. I am just as proud to be a Seneca Indian. And I do not see any reason why I cannot be both. . . .

Lastly, I know it will sound simple and perhaps silly but the truth of the matter is that my people really believe that George Washington read the 1794 Treaty before he signed it, and that he meant exactly what he wrote. For more than 165 years, we Senecas have lived by that document. To us it is more than a contract, more than a symbol; to us the 1794 Treaty is a way of life.

Times have not always been easy for the Seneca people. We have known and we still know poverty and discrimination. But through it all we have been sustained by a pledge of faith, unbroken by the Federal government. Take that pledge away, break our treaty, and I fear that you will destroy the Senecas as an Indian community.

1961

In June representatives of ninety tribes from all over the United States met in Chicago and drafted a "Declaration of Indian Purpose," in which they presented their suggestions for remedying the destructive pressures that had been put upon them by the government. It said, in part:

When our lands are taken for a declared public purpose, scattering our people and threatening our continued existence, it grieves us to be told that a money payment is the equivalent of all the things we surrender. Our forefathers could be generous when all the continent was theirs. They could cast away whole empires for a handful of trinkets for their children. But in our day, each remaining acre is a promise that we will still be here tomorrow. Were we paid a thousand times the market value of our lost holdings, still the payment would not suffice. Money never mothered the Indian people as the land has mothered them, nor have any people become more closely attached to the land, religiously and traditionally. We insist again that this is not special pleading. We ask only that the United States be true to its own traditions and set an example to the world in fair dealing. . . .

When Indians speak of the continent they yielded, they are not referring only to the loss of some millions of acres in real estate. They have in mind that the land supported a universe of things they knew, valued, and loved.

With that continent gone, except for the few poor parcels they

The Cree artist Alfred Young Man strikingly depicts one result of the alienation of the Indians from their lands and the desecration of Indian holy places deplored in the "Declaration of Indian Purpose." Here, a sad-eyed Indian stolidly awaits the arrival of tourists, amid signs of the commercialization of the American countryside. Photograph courtesy of the artist.

still retain, the basis of life is precariously held, but they mean to hold the scraps and parcels as earnestly as any small nation or ethnic group was ever determined to hold identity and survival. . . .

. . . the history and development of America show that the Indian has been subjected to duress, undue influence, unwarranted pressures, and policies which have produced uncertainty, frustration, and despair. Only when the public understands these conditions and is moved to take action toward the formulation and adoption of sound and consistent policies will these destroying factors be removed and the Indian resume his normal growth and make his maximum contribution to modern society.

We believe in the future of a greater America, an America which we were the first to love, where life, liberty, and the pursuit of happiness will be a reality. In such a future, with Indians and all other Americans cooperating, a cultural climate will be created in which the Indian people will grow and develop as members of a free society.

Crow tribal delegates in Washington, D.C. Those who participated in the interview were John Cummins (seated at right of Secretary of the Interior Stewart L. Udall), Edison Real Bird (standing second from left), and Robert Bends (standing second from right). Commissioner of Indian Affairs Philleo Nash stands at extreme left. Courtesy of the U.S. Bureau of Indian Affairs.

1962

John B. Cummins, chairman of the Crow Tribal Council, in an interview published in *Américas*, discussed the results of white encroachment on the Crow reservation, and the appropriation of Crow land.

We had a claim against the U.S. Government for thirty-three million acres of land that was once owned by the Crow tribe and this was the basis for the settlement that we have just received. We are very fortunate that we have won this money from the U.S. government. Now, when I say fortunate, I mean that the Crow Indians are very poor. Today we are living among the white people who have immigrated onto the Crow Indian reservation. The Crow Indians have had to sell their land because they needed the money. If they had financial help before the Crow reservation today would have been intact. . . .

We have some [people] in business, some in farming, and some are in livestock. We know that we can't make farmers or livestock raisers out of all of them, but that is what most of them want to do. Very few of our Indian people have college educations, but those who do want to go into other businesses. . . .

We like to keep our identity as Indians. The objective and the policy of the present tribal government is education. We want education, we want to educate our children to know the ways of the white man, so that they can help themselves as well as helping the Crow tribe in carrying on its own business. We know the Indian can be an equal to the white man if he has the education. For example, Mr. Real Bird is a college graduate. I finished eighth grade, and Mr. Bends is a high school graduate. But we don't like to see our Indians lose their traditions as Crow Indians. We want to be Crow Indians and at the same time we want to be equal to the white population in the rest of the United States. I don't know if you understand that being an Indian, I am proud to be an Indian.

Ben Black Elk loved to tell children about the history of his people. Courtesy of the South Dakota Division of Tourism.

1968

Ben Black Elk, son of the famous Oglala Sioux chief Black Elk, has been called "the most photographed Indian in history." He played featured roles in the movies and posed for thousands of pictures at Mount Rushmore National Park, where he spent many summers telling visiting children of all races the true story of his people. But, more than that, he was deeply concerned about the future of his people. In an article in *Red Cloud Country,* he wrote of the effects of contact with the white men's world on the Sioux people and on himself personally.

Our young people today . . . do not really know who they are or where they belong. So they have no pride. Today there are Indians who are ashamed they are Indians. . . .

We would like to be proud we are Indians, but . . . many schools for Indian children make them ashamed they are Indians. . . . The schools forget these are Indian children. They don't recognize them as Indians, but treat them as though they were white children. . . . This makes for failure, because it makes for confusion. And when the Indian history and the Indian culture is ignored, it makes our children ashamed they are Indians.

I started to school when I was seven years old. I couldn't speak a word of English. I had long hair that hung to my waist, and it was in four braids. When I made progress in school, a braid was cut off to mark my progress. . . .

Martin Luther King said, "I have a dream." But we Indians didn't have to dream. We had the reality. This whole continent was a paradise. We didn't know what a dollar was or what whiskey was. We got along fine. Then the white man came. That was our downfall. Then the persecution started. So, after many years, out of their sorrow and misery, and because they were desperate, some of the Indians danced the Ghost Dance. . . .

It was a prayer that was danced. The Indians were desperate. All they had, the great buffalo herds, everything was all gone. Then someone came along [Jack Wilson, founder of the Ghost Dance religion] and he told the Indians, "I'm the Messiah, I'm Christ." He said the white man had sinned against him and if he would do the Ghost Dance the white man would disappear and the buffalo and all the old warriors would come back. We were to throw all our weapons away. This would happen with no warfare. We just had to dance and sing this Ghost Dance.

They thought it would come, but it never came. Instead we had the massacre at Wounded Knee. They killed the men, women and children. The sadness of this is still in our hearts. . . .

It was there . . . that a beautiful dream died in the snow—a people's dream.

Harold Cardinal discussing Indian problems with Canadian government officials on 18 December 1970. Left to right: Premier Harry Strom, Harold Cardinal, and Jean Chrétien, Minister of Indian Affairs. Provincial Archives of Canada, Edmonton Journal Collection.

1969

Harold Cardinal, a twenty-four-year-old Cree Indian, became a forceful spokesman for Indian rights when he denounced the deliberate exploitation of his people by Canadians in his book, *The Unjust Society: The Tragedy of Canada's Indians.*

> After generations of endless frustration with the Canadian government, our people are tired and impatient. *Before* the Canadian government tries to feed us hypocritical policy statements, more empty promises, more forked tonguistics, our people want, our people, the Indians, demand just settlement of all our treaty and aboriginal rights. Fulfillment of Indian rights by the queen's government must come before there can be further co-operation between the Indians and the government. We demand nothing more. We expect nothing less.
>
> Yes, the prime minister roused our hopes with his talk of a compassionate and just society. Then his minister for Indian affairs told us our problems would vanish if we would become nice, manageable white men like all other Canadians. Just recently, the prime minister himself flicked the other fork in his tongue. In a speech in Vancouver, Mr. Trudeau said, "The federal government is not prepared to guarantee the aboriginal rights of Canada's Indians. . . ."

To the Indians of Canada, the treaties represent an Indian Magna Carta. The treaties are important to us, because we entered into these negotiations with faith, with hope for a better life with honor. We have survived for over a century on little but that hope. Did the white man enter into them with something less in mind? . . .

Our leaders mistakenly thought they were dealing with an honorable people who would do no less than the Indians were doing—bind themselves, bind their people and bind their heirs to honorable contracts. . . .

The treaties were the way in which the white people legitimized in the eyes of the world their presence in our country. . . . There never had been any doubt in the minds of our people that the land in Canada belonged to them. . . .

In the language of the Cree Indians, the Indian reserves are known as *the land that we kept for ourselves or the land that we did not give to the government.* In our language, *skun-gun.* . . .

Our rights are too valuable to surrender to gallic or any other kind of rhetoric, too valuable to be sold for pieces of gold. Words change; the value of money fluctuates, may even disappear; our land will not disappear.

We cannot give up our rights without destroying ourselves as people. If our rights are meaningless, if it is inconceivable that our society have treaties with the white society even though those treaties were signed by honorable men on both sides, in good faith, long before the present government decided to tear them up as worthless scraps of paper, then we as a people are meaningless. We cannot and we will not accept this. We know that as long as we fight for our rights we will survive. If we surrender, we die.

172

David Courchene.
Courtesy of Chief David Courchene.

1969

When Chief David Courchene (Nee-Gha-Ni Bi-Nah-See, "Leading Thunderbird"), president of the Manitoba Indian Brotherhood, addressed a conference of Indians and Métis (offspring of mixed Indian-white marriages) in Winnipeg, he was extremely critical of the results of white control of the Indians in Canada.

A hundred years of submission and servitude, of protectionism and paternalism have created psychological barriers for Indian people that are far more difficult to break down and conquer than are the problems of economic and social poverty. Paternalistic programs of the past, based largely on the idea that we must shelter and protect the ignorant savage, have created complex problems to those who want to shelter and protect themselves.

. . . Where once the Indian roamed, the factories, farms, and dwellings of a European horde block passage. We are dispossessed of our ancient ways and face with life in a city. . . .

We know that we can't turn back the clock. We know that we can't live for long in a wilderness that is fast being ransacked of fish and fur to feed and clothe the luxury-minded dwellers of the city. So, we too must enter the confines of the city and try as best we might to make our way.

But, understand, oh white man; understand, lovely lady dressed in fur! It is hard, very hard, to know that the land that once was ours will never ever again be our hunting grounds. It is hard to bear the crime-filled streets and the liquor-selling bars where once was only peaceful grass and sobriety. We understand that we must change—and we are changing—but remember: it once was our land, our life, and it is hard.

Withdrawing from white society to many Indians means joining the Native American Church and, through peyote-induced visions, developing an inner life that effectively shuts out the ugliness of the everyday world. A watercolor by Ernest Sawbuck entitled Kickapoo Peyote Ceremony. *Courtesy of the Museum of the American Indian, New York City.*

1970

Wilfred Pelletier was born in the Odawa Indian village of Wikwemikong on Manitoulin Island, Ontario. He has written widely on the continuous conflict between Canadian Indians and white people. In an article originally published in *This Magazine is About Schools* and later widely reprinted, he explained the Indian point of view.

> The Indians have fundamentally rejected society as it now is. The Indians are expert at making all programs that the Indian Affairs Branch has ever come up with a failure by withdrawing. . . . We have a society here where we must win. For everything you do you must end up fighting—fighting for your rights, war against poverty, the fight for peace. The whole base of Western culture has an enemy concept. What would happen if you remove an enemy? How then do you defeat somebody who is on your side? I suspect that if you remove the enemy the culture might collapse. The Indian can't fight on your terms. For a start he doesn't even have the numbers, much less the inclination. So he withdraws. And he pays a certain price. He suffers poverty in many ways.
>
> But maybe the future is with the Indian. Marshall McLuhan says that the only people living in the twenty-first century are the Indians, the Eskimos, some French people and the Japanese. All the rest, because they deal with history, live in the nineteenth century because they deal with the past and not the present. The Pan-Indian movement, with the Native American Church, recognizes this and there are various Native American cultures that are moving closer and closer together. It's a spontaneous thing that just happened. . . . It's a movement. And it's made me much more hopeful.

On 8 July 1970, a group of Hopi leaders met with President Nixon to discuss some of the many problems facing the tribe. *National Archives Trust Fund.*

1970

When the Peabody Coal Company, a subsidiary of the Kennecott Copper Company, began strip mining some 65,000 acres of Hopi and Navajo lands, including a section of Black Mesa, a sacred shrine of the Hopis in Arizona, a group called the Hopi Traditional Village Leaders wrote to, and later met with, President Nixon in protest. They accused the whites of insensitivity to Hopi needs, and of desecration of their beliefs through desecration of their lands.

Dear President Nixon,

We, the true and traditional religious leaders, recognized as such by the Hopi People, maintain full authority over all land and life contained within the Western hemisphere. We are granted our stewardship by virtue of our instruction as to the meaning of Nature, Peace, and Harmony as spoken to our People by Him, known to us as Massau'u, the Great Spirit, who long ago provided for us the sacred stone tablets which we preserve to this day. For many generations before the coming of the Navajo, the Hopi People have lived in the sacred place known to you as the Southwest and known to us to be the spiritual center of our continent. Those of us of the Hopi Nation who have followed the path of the Great Spirit without compromise have a message which we are committed, through our prophecy, to convey to you.

The white man, through his insensitivity to the way of Nature, has desecrated the face of Mother Earth. The white man's advanced technological capacity has occurred as a result of his lack of regard for the spiritual path and for the way of all living things. The white man's desire for material possessions and power has blinded him to the pain he has caused Mother Earth by his quest for what he calls natural resources. And the path of the Great Spirit has become difficult to see by almost all men, even by many Indians who have chosen instead to follow the path of the white man. . . .

Today the sacred lands where the Hopi live are being desecrated by men who seek coal and water from our soil that they may create more power for the white man's cities. This must not be allowed to continue for if it does, Mother Nature will react in such a way that almost all men will suffer the end of life as they now know it. The Great Spirit said not to allow this to happen even as it was prophesied to our ancestors. The Great Spirit said not to take from the Earth—not to destroy living things. The Great Spirit, Massau' u, said that man was to live in Harmony and maintain a good clean land for all children to come. All Hopi People and other Indian Brothers are standing on this religious principle and the Traditional Spiritual Unity Movement today is endeavoring to reawaken the spiritual nature in Indian people throughout this land. Your Government has almost destroyed our basic religion which actually is a way of life for all our people in this land of the Great Spirit. We feel that to survive the coming Purification Day, we must return to the basic religious principles and to meet together on this basis as leaders of our people.

Today almost all the prophecies have come to pass. Great roads like rivers pass across the landscape; man talks to man through the cobwebs of telephone lines; man travels along the roads in the sky in his airplanes; two great wars have been waged by those bearing the swastika or the rising sun; man is tampering with the Moon and the stars. Most men have strayed from the path shown us by the Great Spirit. For Massau'u alone is great enough to portray the way back to Him.

It is said by the Great Spirit that if a gourd of ashes is dropped upon the Earth, that many men will die and that the end of this way of life is near at hand. We interpret this as the dropping of atomic bombs on Hiroshima and Nagasaki. We do not want to see this happen to any place or any nation again, but instead we should turn all this energy for peaceful uses, not war.

. We, the religious leaders and rightful spokesmen for the Hopi Independent Nation, have been instructed by the Great Spirit to express the invitation to the President of the United States and all spiritual leaders everywhere to meet with us and discuss the welfare of mankind so that Peace, Unity, and Brotherhood will become part of all men everywhere.

Sincerely,

Thomas Banyacya, for
Hopi Traditional Village Leaders;
Mrs. Mina Lansa, Oraibi [Village]
Claude Kawangyawma, Shungopavy [Village]
Starlie Lomayaktwea, Mushongnovi [Village]
Dan Katchongva, Hotevilla [Village]

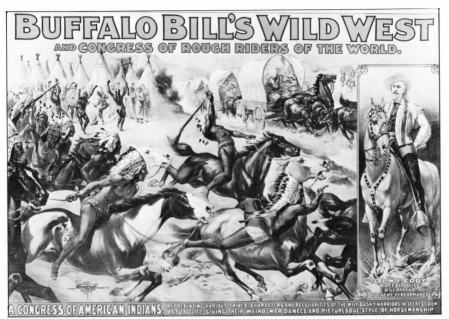

Chief Red Fox was one of several Indians who traveled across the United States and in Europe with Buffalo Bill's Wild West Show. The show's posters were masterpieces of advertising, though not always this dynamic. The show also depicted vignettes of family life among the Indians. Reproduced from the Collections of the Library of Congress.

1971

Red Fox, a Sioux chief, the nephew of Crazy Horse, was born in the foothills of the Big Horn Mountains on 11 June 1870. He traveled widely and knew many celebrities, including Buffalo Bill (with whose troupe he performed), Kaiser Wilhelm II of Germany, King George V of England, Jack London, Will Rogers, and Theodore Roosevelt. His *Memoirs*, published five years before his death in 1976 at the age of 105, were developed from his own notes. They are a vivid commentary on Indian-white relations, and reveal a poignant nostalgia for the world that the white man destroyed.

> When I entered the school I had no thought but that I would spend my life in a tepee and hunt buffalo as my father had. Even by the time I was ready to leave, I had no more than a vague idea of what lay ahead for me, but a magic door had been opened that would take me from the ABC's to calculus; from a tepee lighted with buffalo oil burning in a clay dish, to the electric lights in a penthouse; from messages sent through puffs of smoke made by a blanket over a campfire to a swift interchange by telephone; from the horse to the superjet; and lastly, perhaps most significantly, from the arrow to the hydrogen bomb.
>
> Had I been told in prophecy that I would meet the people who

carved these advances out of dreams and imagination, I would have had no comprehension of what was said; but when I finally met them and moved along with their "progress," I wondered if my elation compared to that of the White man; or did my heritage and lingering love of the past lessen my appreciation for the achievements of another race and the personalities it produced.

I met Thomas Edison and Alexander Graham Bell, and many others who impressed me as great people, but pride in them and their achievements has not overawed me, for I am not convinced that the comforts and advancements which they brought into the world have made people more content and happy than the Indians were through the centuries on the mountains, prairies, and deserts of the primeval, virgin continent.

. . . I have lived a storybook life and am not ungrateful for what the White man has given me, but the ghosts of my ancestors stalk me at times in the dark and congregate around me when I meditate in solitude. Although I have adapted to my environment, like immigrants have done, I am still a native of the wilderness. I did not come to this country in search of riches and freedom, I am as much a part of this country as the insensate rock and the Sequoia tree, as my ancestors were millenniums before me. I would be insensitive if I did not sorrow for the members of my race who are restricted still to the confines of a staked-out reservation—still in the captivity of a foreign civilization. . . . I had been four years in boarding school before returning to my home in the village, and it was a real joy to get back into my parents' tepee, wear mocassins again, and let my hair grow. . . .

During that summer I reverted to the Old Indian ways, but I became restless, for I had absorbed enough of the White man's knowledge to make me want more. In the fall I was sent to the Carlisle Indian School in Pennsylvania. . . .

I learned a lot from books and teachers during the nine years I spent there, and I became acutely aware of who I was and curious about where I came from. These two questions were the main focus of my attention during those years that I was shaking off the clinging vines of the wilderness and taking on the finery of the culture that had adopted me and was trying to make me conform to its patterns of conduct and survival. . . .

The White man's theories of where the Indian came from are a hodgepodge of speculations. . . . This presumption reflects the inborn arrogance of the White man, who believes that he is the first symphonic art work of God, and that if other races were created, it was afterthought—or that the Creator was weary or having a nightmare.

20th-century Wausha tribesmen near the Amazon jungle. Courtesy of FUNAI.

1971

Present-day Brazilian Indian tribes live very much the way their ancestors did before the arrival of the first Portuguese explorers in 1590. Their reactions to modern civilization are strong and definite, and they find many things about it repugnant.

When he became ill, Tawapuh, the son-in-law of the Wausha chief, agreed to fly to São Paulo for medical treatment. He spent a week in the city with an anthropologist, Kenneth S. Brecher, who had lived for two years with the tribe in their home in Xingu National Indian park on the Batavi River. Tawapuh, horrified by what he saw, voluntarily rejected the "benefits" of urban life.

> How could you return to this world after seeing how we live? How can you breathe this foul air or sleep with these noises [the traffic]? How can you eat this food made to have tastes which are not its own? Why would you want to have intercourse with these women who seem afraid to be women and hide themselves and cover their eyes? And who are these men with guns who stand in the paths of the village [the ever-present Brazilian military police]?

This painting by Apache/Pima Carol A. Soati-kee depicts the feelings of estrangement and alienation that affect young Indians who, sent to boarding schools, lose touch with their Indian roots. U.S. Department of the Interior, Indian Arts and Crafts Board.

1973

The Canadian Cree Indians of the James Bay Area were outspoken in their denunciation of the ultimate effects of modernization on their lives. In an interview with Boyce Richardson, a white journalist, Juliette Bearskin, a Canadian Cree, criticized the effects of modern boarding school education on Indian children who will afterward return to resume the traditional tribal way of life.

I have two kids in school. I went to school myself and I understand what they are going through. I went through it for seven years, and before I was sixteen I was asked to leave school so that I could learn the Indian ways.

I had lost most of what I had learned before I went to school. I had to learn it all over again. I had to learn how to check the hooks on the line and set the rabbit snares. When I came back I felt as if I had lost everything during my short time at school, and it is the same with these kids now.

One of my girls is going to school down south. She was thirteen when she left, and the other one is here with us in Fort George. The two are very different. I know they are both learning many other things, and forgetting their Indian ways. We try to teach them when they are both here in the summer. The one who has stayed in Fort George learns our ways much faster than the other one. It is as if she doesn't remember anything she knew before she went down south. She has been slowed down. She seems to have a hard time understanding what we tell her. She's now slow in learning, compared with her sister. I think what caused her to slow down is what she learned at school down south. The sudden change in her environment, the change of cultures, is the cause of it. She must have seen a lot of different things when she was down there. Something must have swayed her. The white man's ways have swayed her.

In the spring of 1973, Indian activists occupied the area around Wounded Knee, South Dakota, and managed to hold off encircling federal forces for weeks. Their aim was to dramatize Indian grievances and call them to the attention of the world. As a manifestation of Pan-Indian solidarity, members of the Edmonton, Alberta, chapter of the American Indian Movement (AIM) marched in support of the action. Provincial Archives of Canada, Edmonton Journal Collection.

1977

In September, over one hundred delegates from non-governmental organizations (organizations affiliated with the United Nations but not official voting bodies) met at the Palais des Nations at Geneva, Switzerland, for an international conference. Among the participants were representatives of sixty Indian nations, and of countries of North, Central, and South America, as well as members of the Human Rights Commission, UNESCO, and forty observers from the United Nations.

Addressing the opening plenary session on 20 September, Russell Means, director of the American Indian Movement, excoriated the United States.

We are people who live in the belly of the monster. The monster being the U.S.A. Every country in the Western Hemisphere follows the lead of the monster. I come not to turn the other cheek. We have turned it now for almost 500 years, and we realize that here in Geneva, this is our first small step into the international community. . . . the President of the U.S.—to show you what a racist he is—[talks] about human rights while my people are suffering genocide. Not only in the U.S. but in the entire Hemisphere—planned genocide by governments. We have brought documents to Geneva that support this charge.

We are approaching the international community this first time for support and assistance to stop not only this rape of our sacred mother earth, but also to stop the genocide of a whole people. A people with international rights backed up especially in North America by treaties between the U.S. and Indian Nations. The U.S., the monster, and its multinational corporations have dictated foreign policy in this world. They no longer care about the future as witnessed by the Dene [Navajo], by my people, by Central and South America. . . .

You see, there is only one color of mankind that is not allowed to participate in the international community, and that color is red. The black, the white, the brown, the yellow—all participate in one form or another. We no longer, until this day, have had a voice within the international community.

Someone once said you can tell the power of a country by the oppression its people will tolerate. No longer are we going to tolerate the monster.

The Alberta delegation, of which Ed Burnstick was a member, at the Non-Governmental Organizations Conference in Geneva, Switzerland. *Courtesy of the International Indian Treaty Council.*

1977

Speaking to the Geneva Conference on behalf of the American Indian Movement in Canada, Ed Burnstick accused the Canadian government of unilaterally decreeing the fate of the Indian people. In his statement to the Conference's Economic Commission he bewailed the manipulation of the Indian through the centuries.

The situation that exists for native people in Canada is that we have been categorized by Canada as Eastern or Western or Northern Canadian Indians, and treaty and non-treaty Indians, registered and non-registered, status Indians and non-status Indians, Métis, half-breed. Economically, each category is affected differently. The responsibility of the Canadian government lies in the control they have gained over all Indian peoples. . . . Indian people have not had a say in the economic situation of their communities. . . . there was a new economic development program set up called the Mid-Canada Corridor. This is the Northern Development Plan. This was a plan to take all economic basis away from Indian people. It involves the Department of Northern Saskatchewan and Northlands in Alberta, the Department of Northern Manitoba where there is a huge hydrodevelopment project going on, and the development programs in Northern Ontario, Quebec, British Columbia and the Territories.

These programs are developed without consultation with the

native people, who are extremely isolated and out of touch. This adds up to genocide against the native people of Canada—culturally and physically. . . . Each province and territory exerts control of the native people within its claimed boundaries. We are affected by such laws as the Migratory Bird Act, and yet in our treaties we have fishing and hunting rights. We have court cases where our people have been put in court for shooting duck to feed their family because it infringed on the Migratory Bird Act. In many areas, there are no jobs, and people must rely on hunting and fishing to survive.

A lot of our land areas have been subject to manipulation. For years, the ranchers have cleared land around the reservations with the cheap labor of native people. Today most of our reserves are faced with dealing with timber mills, paper mills around the reserves. There are power plants which destroy the fish around reserves.

The Government uses "legal" tactics to keep Indian people in poverty. They try to assimilate entire reserves, and have succeeded on some in destroying the language, education and livelihood of the people. . . . The corporations are looking for resources and look more and more to Indian land. We need protection. The death rate has climbed three fold in the last 10 years. Our elders tell us from their oral history, that land that was ceded through treaties included only one foot down, and does not include water and most minerals. The timber and water that exists would be enough for all if shared equally. The world community should think of the human rights of Indian people. We are not saying we do not want to share our resources, but we are saying that we must think of a future where everyone can survive.

Author and lecturer Jamake Highwater has written perceptively and imaginatively about the art, mythology, and history of his people. Photograph by William Coupon, courtesy of Jamake Highwater.

1982

In May, the Manhattan Theatre Club of New York presented a program called Writers in Performance, which featured Indian authors Jamake Highwater (Piitai Sahkomapii, "Eagle Sun"), a Blackfoot/Eastern Band Cherokee, and Maurice Kenny, a Mohawk. In a moving reading, Highwater recounted the Blackfeet version of the beginning of the world from his novel *Anpao: An Indian Odyssey,* which vividly tells the story of the devastating impact of the white man on Indian life, as seen through the eyes of twin brothers, Anpao and Oapna. At one point in the story, Anpao meets a repulsive rider swathed in black, who tells him:

> I am smallpox. . . . I come from far away . . . where the great water is and then far beyond it. I am a friend of the Big Knives who have brought me; they are my people.

And smallpox rides lugubriously off to bring to the Indians the lethal disease that so devastated their tribes.

Notes and Sources

CHAPTER 1—THE 16TH CENTURY

Samuel Drake, *The Book of the Indians of North America* (Boston: Drake, 1833), p. 44.
Pietro Martire d'Anghiera, *The Historie of the West Indies*, trans. M. Lok (London: Hess, c. 1625), p. 70.
Maud W. Makemson, *The Book of the Jaguar Priest* (New York: Schuman, 1951), p. 128.
Op. cit., pp. 128–29.
Bernardino de Sahagún, *Florentine Codex: General History of the Things of New Spain*, trans. Arthur J. O. Anderson and Charles E. Dibble, 12 vols. (Santa Fe, N.M.: University of Utah Press and the School of American Research, 1950–59), vol. 12. Reprinted with permission of the University of Utah Press and the School of American Research. © 1975 by the University of Utah Press.
Ibid.
W. H. Prescott, *History of the Conquest of Mexico and History of the Conquest of Peru* (New York: Modern Library, 1936), vol. 2, p. 940.
Garcilaso de la Vega, *Royal Commentaries of the Incas, and General History of Peru* (Austin: University of Texas Press, 1966), pt. 2, p. 675.
"The Gentleman of Elvas," in Justin Winsor, *A Narrative and Critical History of America*, 8 vols. (Boston: Houghton, Mifflin, 1884–89).
Girolamo Benzoni, *Historia Novi Orbis* (Venice, 1565), vol. 2, ch. 16.
Claude d'Abbeville, *Histoire de la mission des pères capucins en l'isle de Maragnan et terres circonfines ou est traicte des singularitez admirable et des moeurs merveilleuses des indiens habitans de ce pais* (Paris, 1614).
Girolamo Benzoni, *La historia del mondo nuovo* (Venice: Rampazetto, 1565), pp. 48–49.
Hans Staden, *Wahrhaftige Historie und Bescreibung eyner Landtschafft der Wilden, Nacketen, Grimmigen, Menschfresser Leuten in der Newen Welt America gelegen* (Marpurg, 1557), pp. 457–58.
Jean de Léry, *Histoire d'un voyage faict en la terre du Bresil, autrement dite Amérique* (1578), ed. Paul Gaffard, 2 vols. (Paris, 1880), p. 174.
José de Anchieta, *Cartas, informações, fragmentos historicos e sermões*, ed. Antonio de Alcantara Machado (Rio de Janeiro, 1937), pp. 374–75.
Ramirez to Phillip II, in James Lockhart and Enrique Otte, *Letters and People of the Spanish Indies* (New York: Cambridge University Press, 1976), pp. 165–71.
Felipe Guzmán Poma de Ayala, *La primera nueva corónica y buen gobierno*, 1587 (Paris: Institut d'Ethnologie, 1936).
Michel Eyquem de Montaigne, *Les Essais* (Paris: Presses Universitaires de France, 1965), bk. 1, ch. 31, pp. 213–14.
Dominique de Gourgues, "La Reprinse de la Florida," in Henri Ternaux-Compans, *Voyages, rélations et mémoires originaux pour servir a l'histoire de la découverte de l'Amérique* (Paris, 1837–41), vol. 20, p. 329.

CHAPTER 2—THE 17TH CENTURY

Samuel de Champlain, *Les Voyages . . .* (Paris, 1603).
Samuel G. Goodrich, *Lives of Celebrated American Indians* (Boston: Bradbury, Soden, 1843), pp. 179–80.
Francis Parkman, *The Pioneers of New France in the Old World* (Boston: Little, Brown, 1930).
Yves d'Evreux, *Suite de l'histoire . . . 1613 et 1614* (Paris, 1615).
Samuel Purchas, *The Pilgrims* (London: Hakluyt Society, 1626), vol. 19, pp. 117–18.
Andrew A. White, *A Relation of Maryland* (Ann Arbor: Michigan University Microfilms, 1966), pp. 35–36.
Herbert Milton Sylvester, *Indian Wars of New England* (Cleveland: Clark, 1910), vol. 1, p. 386.
John Tebbel and Keith Jennison, *The American Indian Wars* (New York: Harper, 1960), p. 20.
Pierre François Xavier de Charlevoix, *Histoire et description generale de la Nouvelle France* (Paris: Giffart, 1744), vol. 1.
Edmund B. O'Callaghan and F. Berthold, eds., *Documents Relative to the Colonial History of the State of New York* (Albany, N.Y.: Weed, Parsons, 1856–57), vol. 13, p. 109.
Edward Johnson, *A History of New England* (Louisville, Ky.: Lost Cause Press, 1957), p. 9.
Chrestien Le Clercq, *New Relation of Gaspesia, with the Customs and Religion of the Gaspesian Indians*, ed. and trans. William F. Ganong (Toronto: Champlain Society, 1910), pp. 104–06.
Samuel Smith, *The Dutch History of New Jersey* (New York: Hurst, 1886), p. 101–2.
C. Hale Sipe, *The Indian Chiefs of Pennsylvania* (1927; reprint, New York: Arno, 1971), pp. 60–61.
Cadwallader Colden, *The History of the Five Indian Nations of Canada* (1727; reprint, Ithaca, N.Y.: Cornell University Press, 1958), pp. 54–56.
Edmund B. O'Callaghan, *The Documentary History of the State of New York* (Albany, N.Y.: Weed, Parsons, 1847), pp. 401–3.
Lahontan, *Voyages* (The Hague, 1703), vol. 2, p. 182.
Colden, *Five Indian Nations*, pp. 89–91.
Lahontan, *New Voyages to North America*, ed. and trans. R. Thwaites (Chicago: McClurg, 1905), vol. 2, p. 533.
William Beauchamp, *History of the Iroquois of New York* (Albany, N.Y.: New York State Museum, Bulletin 78, Archeology 9, 1905), p. 117.

CHAPTER 3—THE 18TH CENTURY

The Annals of Queen Anne, 1710 (The New York Public Library, microfilm).
Le Page du Pratz, *Histoire de la Louisiane . . .* (Paris, 1758).
Samuel Drake, *The Aboriginal Races of North America* (New York: Hurst, 1880), bk. 4, pp. 368–69.
Op. cit., pp. 370–71.
Cadwallader Colden, *The History of the Five Nations of Canada*, 3d ed. (London: 1755), vol. 2, pp. 18–24.
Beauchamp, *Iroquois of New York*, p. 175.
Tebbel and Jennison, *The American Indian Wars*, pp. 66–67.
John Tebbel, *The Compact History of the Indian Wars* (New York: Hawthorn, 1966), p. 40.

O'Callaghan, *History of the State of New York,* p. 572ff.

James H. Perkins and J. M. Peck, *Annals of the West* (St. Louis: Albach, 1851), p. 104.

Tebbel and Jennison, *The American Indian Wars,* p. 87.

John Heckewelder, *Narrative of the Mission of the United Brethren Among the Delaware and Mohecan Indians* (Philadelphia: McCarty and David, 1757), pp. 61–64.

Thomas Jefferson, *Notes on the State of Virginia* (Boston: Lilly and Wait, 1832), p. 66.

Benjamin Franklin, *Two Tracts, Information to those Who Would Remove to America, and Remarks Concerning the Savages of North America,* 3d ed. (London, Stockdale, 1794), pp. 28–29.

Francis Whiting Halsey, *The Old New York Frontier* (1901; reprint, Port Washington, N.Y.: Friedman, 1963), pp. 155–56.

Samuel Drake, *Biography and History of the Indians of North America* (Boston: Mussey, 1844), pp. 146–48.

John Heckewelder, *An Account of the History, Manners and Customs, of the Indian Nations, Who Once Inhabited Pennsylvania and the Neighbouring States,* Transactions of the Historical and Literary Committee, American Philosophical Society (Philadelphia, 1819), pp. 80–81.

Drake, *Biography and History of the Indians of North America,* pp. 608–11.

American State Papers, 5.

John D. Brown, *Old Frontiers* (Kingsport, Tenn.: Southern Publishers, 1938).

CHAPTER 4—THE 19TH CENTURY

Drake, *Biography and History of the Indians of North America,* pp. 594–96.

William L. Stone, *The Life of Joseph Brant,* 2 vols. (Albany: Munsell, 1864), vol. 2, p. 281.

Drake, *The Book of the Indians of North America,* pp. 100–101.

Katherine C. Turner, *Red Men Calling on the Great White Father* (Norman: University of Oklahoma Press, 1951), pp. 48–49.

Goodrich, *Lives of Celebrated American Indians,* pp. 310–12.

Francis A. Chardon, *Chardon's Journal at Fort Clark 1834–1839,* ed. Annie H. Abel (Pierre, S.D.: Department of History of the State of South Dakota, 1932) pp. 124–25.

Jay David, *The American Indian: The First Victim* (New York: Morrow, 1972). © 1972 by Jay David, pp. 105–6.

W. C. Vanderwerth, comp., *Indian Oratory* (Norman: University of Oklahoma Press, 1971), pp. 118–22.

Clarence B. Bagley, "Chief Seattle and Angeline," *Washington Historical Quarterly,* vol. 22, October 1931, pp. 252–55.

Big Eagle, "Big Eagle's Story of the Sioux Outbreak of 1862," *Minnesota Historical Society Collections,* vol. 6 (1894), pp. 382–400.

New York Times, 30 October 1867, p. 1.

Norman B. Wiltsey, *Brave Warriors* (Caldwell, Idaho: Caxton, 1963), p. 24.

Commissioner of Indian Affairs, annual report, in *Executive Documents,* 1869–70 (Washington, D.C.: Government Printing Office, 1870), vol. 3, p. 448.

New York Times, 17 June 1870, p. 1.

Proceedings of Commission Appointed to Obtain Certain Concessions from the Sioux Indians, 44th Cong., 2d sess., Senate Executive Document 9, p. 38.

Wiltsey, *Brave Warriors,* p. 315.

E. A. Brininstool, *Crazy Horse* (Los Angeles: Wetzel, 1949), pp. 53–61.

Chief Joseph, "An Indian's View of Indian Affairs," *North American Review,* vol. 26 (April 1879), pp. 415–33.

Report of Conference . . . between General Crook and the Hostile Chiricahua Chiefs, 51st Cong., 1st sess. Senate Executive Document 88, pp. 11–12.

Stanley Vestal, *New Sources of Indian History, 1850–91,* (Norman: University of Oklahoma Press, 1934), pp. 382–84.

CHAPTER 5—THE 20TH CENTURY

Congressional Record, 64th Cong., 1st sess. 12 May 1916, pp. 7843–45.

Wiltsey, *Brave Warriors,* p. 228.

Syndicated newspaper columns, 5 February 1928; 4 May 1930.

Luther Standing Bear, *Land of the Spotted Eagle* (Lincoln: University of Nebraska Press, 1933), pp. 165–66, 247–48, 258–59.

Ruth Muskrat Bronson, "Shall We Repeat Indian History in Alaska?" *Indian Truth* (January–April 1947), pp. 1–9.

The Rotarian (August 1954), pp. 27–28.

George D. Heron to the House Subcommittee on Indian Affairs, reprinted in *The Kinzua Dam Controversy* (Philadelphia: Philadelphia Yearly Meeting of Friends, 1961), pp. 8–10.

From "The Declaration of Indian Purpose," American Indian Chicago Conference, 13–20 June 1961.

Américas (September 1962), pp. 7, 9.

Ben Black Elk, "How it Feels to be an Indian in the White Man's World," *Red Cloud Country* (April–June 1968), pp. 1–3.

Harold Cardinal, *The Unjust Society: The Tragedy of Canada's Indians* (Edmonton: Hurtig, 1969), pp. 27–30.

Courtesy of Chief David Courchene.

Wilfred Pelletier, in *This Book is About Schools,* ed. Satu Repo (New York: Pantheon, 1970), pp. 18–32.

Reprinted in T. J. McLuhan, *Touch the Earth* (New York: Promontory, 1971), pp. 170–71. Reprinted by permission of Thomas Banyacya.

Chief Red Fox, *Memoirs of Chief Red Fox* (New York: McGraw-Hill, 1971), pp. 98–103.

Orlando Villas Boas and Claudio Villas Boas, *Xingu: The Indians, Their Myths* (New York: Farrar, Straus & Giroux, 1973), p. xi.

Boyce Richardson, *Strangers Devour the Land* (New York: Knopf, 1976), p. 185–86.

Chronicles of American Indian Protest (New York: Council on Interracial Books for Children, 1979), p. 349. Reproduced by permission of Russell Means.

Op. cit., pp. 352–53. Reproduced by permission of Ed Burnstick.

Jamake Highwater, *Anpao: An American Indian Odyssey* (New York: Harper & Row, 1977), p. 24.

Reading List

(In addition to books, articles, and captions credited in source notes and captions)

Anderson, Eva G. *Chief Seattle*. Caldwell, Idaho: Caxton, 1951.
Armstrong, Virginia. *I Have Spoken*. Chicago: Swallow, 1971.
Bancroft, Hubert H. *The Conquest of Mexico*. New York, 1883.
Barck, Oscar T., and Hugh Talmage Lefler. *Colonial America*. New York: Macmillan, 1958.
Beal, Allen. *I Will Fight No More Forever*. Seattle: University of Washington Press, 1963.
Bennett, Charles E., comp. *Settlement of Florida*. Gainesville: University of Florida Press, 1968.
Benson, Elizabeth P. *The Maya World*. Rev. ed. New York: Crowell, 1977.
Black Hawk. *An Autobiography* (1834). Urbana: University of Illinois Press, 1955.
Bolton, Herbert E. *The Spanish Borderlands*. New Haven: Yale University Press, 1921.
Bradford, William. *Of Plymouth Plantation*. Ed. S. E. Morison. New York: Knopf, 1966.
Brebner, John B. *The Explorers of North America*. New York: Meridian, 1955.
Brown, Dee. *Bury My Heart at Wounded Knee*. New York: Holt, Rinehart & Winston, 1970.
Brown, Dee, and Martin F. Schmitt. *Fighting Indians of the West*. New York: Ballantine, 1948.
Brown, John P. *Old Frontiers* (1938). New York: Arno, 1971.
Burt, Jesse, and Robert B. Ferguson. *Indians of the Southeast, Then and Now*. Nashville, Tenn.: Abingdon, 1973.
Catlin, George. *Letters and Notes on the Manners, Customs and Condition of the North American Indians* (1841). 2 vols. Minneapolis: Ross & Haines, 1965.
Champlain, Samuel de. *Works*. Ed. H. P. Biggar. Toronto: Champlain Society, 1922–23.
Cieza de León, Piedro. *The Second Part of the Chronicle of Peru*. Trans. and ed. with notes and introduction by Clements R. Markham. London: Hakluyt Society, 1883.
Collis, Maurice. *Cortés and Montezuma*. New York: Avon, 1954.
Columbus, Christopher. *Journal of the First Voyage to America*. Introduction by Van Wyck Brooks. New York: Boni, 1924.
Costo, Rupert, and Jeannette Henry. *Indian Treaties, Two Centuries of Dishonor*. San Francisco: Indian Historian Press, 1977.
Debo, Angie. *A History of the Indians of the United States*. Norman: University of Oklahoma Press, 1970.
Deloria, Vine, Jr. *Custer Died for Your Sins*. New York: Macmillan, 1969.
De Rosier, Arthur H. J. *The Removal of the Choctaw Indians*. New York: Harper & Row, 1972.
Díaz del Castillo, Bernal. *Discovery and Conquest of Mexico*. New York: Farrar, Straus & Cudahy, 1956.
Dockstader, Frederick J. *Great North American Indians*. New York: Van Nostrand Reinhold, 1977.
Drake, Benjamin. *The Life and Adventures of Black Hawk*. 7th ed. Cincinnati, Ohio: Applegate, 1851.
Driver, Harold W. *The Americans on the Eve of Discovery*. Englewood Cliffs, N.J.: Prentice-Hall, 1964.
Dupuy, R. Ernest, and Trevor N. Dupuy. *The Compact History of the Revolutionary War*. New York: Hawthorn, 1963.
Eccles, W. J. *France in America*. New York: Harper & Row, 1972.
Eckert, Allan W. *The Frontiersman*. Boston: Little, Brown, 1967.
Every, Dale. *Disinherited: The Lost Birthright of the American Indian*. New York: Morrow, 1968.
Farb, Peter. *Man's Rise to Civilization*. . . . New York: Dutton, 1961.
Fiske, John. *New France and New England*. Boston: Houghton, Mifflin, 1902.
Forbes, Jack D. *The Indian in America's Past*. Englewood Cliffs, N.J.: Prentice-Hall, 1964.
Foreman, Carolyn. *Indians Abroad, 1493–1938*. Norman: University of Oklahoma Press, 1943.
Foreman, Grant. *Indian Removal*. Norman: University of Oklahoma Press, 1917.
Georgakas, Dan. *Red Shadows: The History of Native Americans from 1600 to 1900, from the Desert to the Pacific Coast*. Garden City, N.Y.: Zenith Books, 1973.
Graymont, Barbara. *The Iroquois in the American Revolution*. Syracuse, N.Y.: Syracuse University Press, 1972.
Gurko, Miriam. *Indian America: The Black Hawk War*. New York: Crowell, 1970.
Hakluyt, Richard. *The Principal Navigations*. 8 vols. New York, 1826.
Haring, C. H. *The Spanish Empire in America*. New York: Harcourt, Brace & World, 1947.
Helps, Arthur. *The Spanish Conquest of America*. New York: Harper, 1856.
Hemming, John. *The Conquest of the Incas*. New York: Harcourt Brace Jovanovich, 1973.
———. *Red Gold: The Conquest of the Brazilian Indians, 1500–1760*. Cambridge, Mass.: Harvard University Press, 1978.
Herrera, Antonio. *Historia General de los hechos de los Castellanos* . . . Buenos Aires: Guaranía, 1944–47.
Hodge, Frederick Webb, ed. *Handbook of American Indians North of Mexico*. 2 vols. New York: Pageant, 1959.
Honour, Hugh. *The European Vision of America*. Cleveland: Cleveland Museum of Art, 1975.
———. *The New Golden Land*. New York: Random House, 1971.
Illick, Joseph E. *Colonial Pennsylvania*. New York: Scribner, 1976.
Irving, Washington. *Life and Voyages of Christopher Columbus*. New York: Putnam, 1851.
Jahoda, Gloria. *The Trail of Tears*. New York: Holt, Rinehart & Winston, 1975.
Jameson, J. Franklin, ed. *Narratives of New Netherlands, 1609–1664*. New York, 1909.
Johnson, Edward. *A History of New England*. Louisville, Ky.: Lost Cause Press, 1957. Microfiche.
Johnson, William Weber. *Cortés*. Boston: Little, Brown, 1975.
Joseph, Chief. "An Indian's View of Indian Affairs." *North American Review*. Vol. 128 (April 1979): 415–33.
Josephy, Alvin, Jr. *The American Heritage Book of Indians*. New York: Simon & Schuster, 1961.
———. *The Indian Heritage of America*. New York: Knopf, 1970.
———. *The Patriot Chiefs*. New York: Viking, 1961.
———. *Red Power: The American Indians' Fight for Freedom*. New York: American Heritage Press, 1971.
Julien, Ch.-André. *Les voyages de découverte et les premiers établissements*. Paris, 1948.
Las Casas, Bartolomé de. *Historia de las Indias*. Ed. Gonzalo de Reparaz. Madrid, 1927.
———. *Narratio Regionum*. Oppenheim, 1614.

León-Portilla, Miguel, ed. *The Broken Spears. The Aztec Account of the Conquest of Mexico.* Boston: Beacon, 1962.
Lockhart, James. *The Men of Cajamarca.* Austin: University of Texas Press, 1972.
———. *Spanish Peru 1532–1560.* Madison: University of Wisconsin Press, 1968.
Lowery, Woodbury. *The Spanish Settlements.* 2 vols. New York: Russell & Russell, 1959.
McLuhan, T. C. *Touch the Earth.* New York: Promontory, 1971.
Margry, Pierre. *Découvertes et établissements des français dans l'ouest et dans le sud de l'Amérique septentrionale (1614–1754).* 6 vols. Paris, 1867.
Mooney, James. *Historical Sketch of the Cherokee.* Chicago: Aldine Press, 1975.
Moquin, Wayne, and Charles Van Doren, eds. *Great Documents in American Indian History.* New York: Praeger, 1973.
Morison, Samuel E. *Admiral of the Ocean Seas.* 2 vols. Boston: Little, Brown, 1942.
———. *The European Discovery of America: Northern Voyages.* New York: Oxford University Press, 1971.
———. *The European Discovery of America: Southern Voyages.* New York: Oxford University Press, 1974.
———. *Samuel de Champlain, Father of New France.* Boston: Atlantic Monthly Press, 1972.
Nammack, Georgiana C. *Fraud, Politics, and the Dispossession of the Indians.* Norman: University of Oklahoma Press, 1969.
Norman, Charles. *Discoverers of America.* New York: Crowell, 1968.
Oehler, C. M. *The Great Sioux Uprising.* New York: Oxford University Press, 1959.
Oviedo y Valdés, Gonzalo Fernández de. *Natural History of the West Indies.* Trans. and ed. Sterling A. Stoudemire. Chapel Hill: University of North Carolina Press, 1959.
Padden, R. C. *The Humming Bird and the Hawk: Conquest and Sovereignty in the Valley of Mexico, 1503–1541.* Columbus: Ohio State University Press, 1967.
Parker, Arthur C. *History of the Seneca Indians (1926).* Port Washington, N. Y.: Friedman, 1967.
Parkman, Francis. *The Conspiracy of Pontiac.* New York: Collier, 1962.
Parry, J. H. *The Spanish Seaborne Empire.* New York: Knopf, 1966.
Peckham, Howard. *Pontiac and the Indian Uprising.* 2d ed. New York: Russell, 1970.
Pizarro, Pedro. Ed. P. A. Means. *Relation of the Discovery and Conquest of the Kingdoms of Peru.* London: Hakluyt Society, 1921.
Prescott, W. H. *History of the Conquest of Mexico and History of the Conquest of Peru.* New York: Modern Library, 1936.
Quinn, David Beers. *England and the Discovery of America.* New York: Knopf, 1973.
Richardson, Boyce. *Strangers Devour the Land.* New York: Knopf, 1976.
Sahagún, Bernardino de. *Historia general de las cosas de Nueva España.* Mexico: Porrua, 1969.
Sánchez-Barba, Mario Hernández. *Historia universal de América.* Madrid: Guadarrama, 1963. Vol. 2.
Sandoz, Mari. *Crazy Horse.* New York: Knopf, 1942.
Sawvel, Franklin B. *Logan the Mingo.* Boston: Badger, Gorham Press, 1921.
Schoolcraft, Henry R. *Information Respecting the History, Condition and Prospects of the Indian Tribes of the United States.* 6 vols. Philadelphia: Lippincott, Grambo, 1853.
Spicer, Edward H. *A Short History of the Indians of the United States.* New York: Van Nostrand, 1969.
Steiner, Stan. *The New Indians.* New York: Colophon, 1968.
Tebbel, John. *The Compact History of the Indian Wars.* New York: Hawthorn, 1966.
Thevet, André. *La cosmographie universelle.* Paris, 1575.
Thwaites, Reuben Gold, ed. *The Jesuit Relations and Allied Documents . . . 1610–1791.* 73 vols. Cleveland: Burroughs, 1896–1901.
Trelease, Allen W. *Indian Affairs in Colonial New York.* Ithaca: Cornell University Press, 1960.
Tyler, Daniel, ed. *Red Men and Hat Wearers. Viewpoints in Indian History. Papers from the Colorado State University Conference on Indian History.* Boulder, Colo.: Pruett, 1976.
Tyler, Lyman S. *A History of Indian Policy.* U.S. Department of the Interior. Washington, D.C.: BIA, 1973.
Vaughan, Alden T. *New England Frontier* (1620–75). Boston: Little, Brown, 1965.
Vestal, Stanley. *New Sources of Indian History.* Norman: University of Oklahoma Press, 1934.
Vogel, Virgil J. *This Country was Ours. A Documentary History of the American Indian.* New York: Harper & Row, 1972.
Wallace, Anthony F. C. *The Death and Rebirth of the Seneca.* New York: Knopf, 1970.
———. *King of the Delawares: Teedyuscung 1700–1763.* Philadelphia: University of Pennsylvania Press, 1949.
Whittaker, Arthur P. *The Spanish American Frontier 1783–1795.* Gloucester, Mass.: Peter Smith, 1962.
Wilson, Edmund. *Apologies to the Iroquois.* New York: Farrar, Straus & Cudahy, 1959.
Winsor, Justin, ed. *A Narrative and Critical History of America.* 8 vols. Boston: Houghton, Mifflin, 1884–89.
Woodward, Grace Steele. *Pocahontas.* Norman: University of Oklahoma Press, 1969.
Xeres, Francisco de. *La historia verdadera de la conquista.* Seville, 1535.

Index

Figures in italics refer to illustrations

191